UNCLAIMED *Blessings*

Accessing God's Goodness for Your Life

DIANA & HANY ASAAD

Relentless Publications

ISBN-13: 978-0-9983999-0-4

DEDICATION

For Lily, Grace, and Hannah who are our greatest blessings. We pray that you continue to seek God for His best for your lives.

Love,

Mom and Dad

CONTENTS

Introduction

"The Lord isn't really being slow about His promises, as some people think. No, he is being patient for your sake. He does not want anyone to be destroyed but wants everyone to repent." 2 Peter 3:9 NLT

A blessed life might not be what you expect. Yet it will be more than you ever imagined it could be. Through these pages we want to help guide you in understanding and embracing God's goodness for your life. By shattering misconceptions and redefining concepts, we will show you how to bring healing and transformation to your life in the most unexpected way. Join us as we explore God's promises and will for us as believers.

Maybe you have felt a more fulfilled life exists just outside of your reach. Or possibly you have sensed that God has more in store for you, but you are unable to acquire it. Wouldn't it be nice if we understood and could unlock whatever is hindering these blessings? Or, perhaps we never claimed what rightfully belongs to us. If you have felt any of these things you are not alone. Many people feel the very same way.

An Egyptian story tells about a poor man long ago who got a call from an attorney representing the estate of the man's rich uncle who had passed away. Because there were no other heirs to his fortune, this man stood to gain the riches. The meager man tidied up and gathered himself to go to the lawyer's office. With lavish dreams in hand he entered in. The attorney had the humble fellow sign some documents, handed him a piece of paper, and asked him to leave. Crushed, the nephew left and started the long walk home. Being a simple man, he could not read or write, and all he was left with was a deflated dream. He folded the piece of paper and carefully placed it in his pocket. Little did he know that the piece of paper he tucked away was a check for an incredible amount of money. The man resorted to living a life of unmet expectations and unfulfilled potential because he did not know how to claim what was rightfully his. How often do we do the same?

Many blessings remain unclaimed in our lives. It's conceivable that like the poor man in the story, we don't know that we have the right to claim God's blessings. Another possibility is that we are looking in the wrong places.

Imagine with me: Someone went to the doctor's office and then to a grocery store. At the grocery store, they discovered that they lost their wallet at the doctor's office. So they went to the grocery store's lost and found looking for it. That's not very smart, right? Sometimes we do the same exact thing. We look for blessings in the world that are found only in God's Word.

We know that God's will is for His children to prosper and be blessed. Would we hold something good from our children? How about our Heavenly Father? He has so much for us. His will is for us to go from glory to glory and from power to power. Yesterday's blessings are not good enough for today, and surely, today's blessings are not good enough for tomorrow. "Now the Lord is the Spirit; and where the Spirit of the Lord is, there is liberty. But we all, with unveiled face, beholding as in a mirror the glory of the Lord, are being transformed into the same image from glory to glory, just as by the Spirit of the Lord" (2 Corinthians 3:17-18 NKJV).

So how can we receive God's blessings? Only when God presents them as a gift through Jesus Christ. We were saved "by grace, through faith", and we must live "by grace, through faith". This is the way to blessing. We have been redeemed.

The word redeem means to set someone free by paying a price for his freedom. As a result of what Christ has done for us, we are saved from the curse of judgment and receive the blessing of grace. When you receive Christ, you are not only redeemed from something, but *for* something.

The ultimate blessing is God living in you. The promise of the Spirit means that you can practice the presence of Christ, the character of Christ, and develop the fruits of the Spirit, if you will.

Through these pages, we want to help you examine yourself and see what God wants to develop in your life. As we journey closer in our relationship with Jesus, we begin to see His goodness unfold in our lives, and we want to help make this a blatant reality in your life.

Too often Christians start from a perspective of unbelief or doubt. This is contrary to God's Word. By changing our position and therefore our opinions we begin to understand why God wants to bless us.

How to Use This Book:

Ponder This:

This section provides questions from the chapter to develop the concepts and help take them from head knowledge to heart knowledge.

Practical Practice:

This section helps you to take the concepts and make them applicable to your everyday life.

Pray:

This section provides a prayer at the end of each chapter to help vocalize the concept to God in a relevant way.

SECTION 1
Foundations

CHAPTER 1

A Faithful Foundation

"But blessed is the one who trusts in the Lord, whose confidence is in him. They will be like a tree planted by the water that sends out its roots by the stream. It does not fear when heat comes; its leaves are always green. It has no worries in a year of drought and never fails to bear fruit." Jeremiah 17:7-8 NIV

While sitting in my car, I was overcome with emotion. My world seemed to be crashing down around me. The "comparison game" had taken a toll on my outlook, and I was overwhelmed with the feeling that I was all alone in this world. A desperate cry rang out from my heart and spilled out of my mouth as I asked God if even *He* had forgotten me. I was tired. Tired of comparing. Tired of not measuring up. Tired of never having enough. Tired of the rat race that had become my life. I raised my phone in anger and protested. Once again I turned my frustration to God. "There is no one who cares!" I declared. Suddenly my phone rang. I was surprised that an acquaintance was calling me but even more shocked at the questions that came rushing at me. "Are you all right? Is your family all right? Is your health okay?" These three areas constituted today's battle with God. How could she know? She barely knew me. She answered as if I had asked audibly. "I was praying and you came to mind, and I felt I needed to call and check on you." I was done. God had answered my unworthy prayers and made Himself known to me once again.

Have you played the comparison game? You know, that feeling that others around you get what you deserve? Do you think that promotion was meant for you? Are you struggling in your finances while everyone else seems to have money to spare? Are your friends having babies while you wait? Do you have tumultuous relationships while social media shows perfect couples and families? Why do those around you appear to have God's abundant blessings while discontentment seems to define you? Are you the problem? Is God the problem?

Maybe the problem lies with your not understanding the blessings God has in store for you.

Many people have an incorrect concept of God that hinders them from coming close to Him and receiving what Jesus' death and resurrection purchased for them. I was one of those people, quick to judge God's goodness to those around me while feeling that I didn't measure up. Yet, the truth is God loves every person, and He wants good for them. Through these pages we want to share with you how to understand the goodness of God and the blessings He desires to provide you. With this understanding comes freedom from a mundane life of painful comparisons. He wants to bless you. It's His nature.

Why do you suppose the Bible from Old Testament to New would so strongly emphasize the simple truth that *God is good*? That God is good is a foundational truth of our faith in Him, yet we grapple with applying the concept to everyday life.

Is God Good?

The more we know about God's goodness, the more we can trust Him. The more we trust Him, the more easily we can put our lives in His hands. Only by placing our lives in His hands can we open the way for Him to save us, to bless us and work through us so His will can be done on earth as it is in Heaven. God wants to bless you physically. He wants to bless you financially. The Lord wants to bless your relationships and your work. He wants to give you the desires of your heart. As you accept this revelation of God's goodness, you will receive from Him all that you need.

Author Randy Alcorn discusses this concept as well. He says that abundance isn't God's provision for us to live in luxury, but rather, His provision for me to help others live. God trusts us with His money not to build our own kingdom on earth, but to build His kingdom in Heaven. When our attitudes shift from a "me" mindset to a "we" mentality, we begin to unpack why God wants to bless us. Our Heavenly Father wants to use us to build His Heavenly kingdom. It's our privilege to participate when we allow God to use us for His glory.

We've all heard someone say, "I've been blessed by God," usually in relation to success, health, family, wealth, or a job. Some athletes say this after winning a big game or successful actors proclaiming God's goodness while being interviewed. Everyone wants to claim God's blessing.

The common understanding of "blessed by God" is that He gives us good things. In this respect, we can say that God's blessing is on everyone, believers and unbelievers alike. Matthew 5:45 says that the Father who is in the Heavens causes His sun to rise on the evil and the good and sends rain on the just and unjust. However, God has certain blessings that are reserved for His children.

You must realize and accept that being blessed includes far more than having money. Financial prosperity is only one small portion of the blessings God has in store for His children. But does God's blessing pertain *only* to material things? Though these are included, thinking of God's blessing as mainly material gifts severely limits our understanding of what is in God's heart for us as believers. So let's look at the fuller meaning of being blessed by God.

What is Rightfully Yours?

Many Christians simply don't know what is rightfully theirs. A fundamental truth we need to understand is that none of us deserves His blessing. We cannot earn it. Blessings flow from His grace toward us. "From the fullness of his grace we have all received one blessing after another" John 1:16 (NIV). And although we don't deserve it, God enjoys blessing His children and wants to bless you! "I will enjoy blessing them. With all my heart and soul I will faithfully plant them in this land" Jeremiah 32:41 (GW).

The next truth to understanding what is rightfully yours is that God promises to bless you IF you follow His instructions. Every promise has a principle; there's a condition attached. "If you fully obey the LORD your God and carefully keep all his commands that I am giving you today, the LORD your God will set you high above all the nations of the world. [2] You will experience all these blessings if you obey the LORD your God: [3] Your towns and your fields will be blessed. [4] Your children and your crops will be blessed. The offspring of your herds and flocks will be blessed. [5] Your fruit baskets and breadboards will be blessed. [6] Wherever you go and whatever you do, you will be blessed. [8] The LORD will guarantee a blessing on everything you do and will fill your storehouses with grain. The LORD your God will bless you in the land he is giving you"

Deuteronomy 28:2-6, 8 (NLT).

God wants to bless you in front of others as a testimony. "How great is the goodness you have stored up for those who fear you. You lavish it on those who come to you for protection, blessing them before the watching world" Psalm 31:19 (NLT).

Many Christians think they must settle for being sick, poor or discouraged. They say, "This is just the way it is. I can't do anything about it." They don't know that Jesus Christ has redeemed them from these situations. Some choose to settle for less than God's best. We are going on a journey through this book you are holding so that you are able to press into all His best for your life.

At the back of this book we have a list of one-hundred blessings that are rightfully yours as a believer if you follow God's will for your life. These pages are a great place to start seeing God's promises and asking for His will to unfold in your life.

Do You Take Exception?

A police officer can't effectively enforce the law if he thinks that sometimes it's okay to speed and other times it's not. Is it okay to rob a bank sometimes but other times not? Is it permissible to murder occasionally? No, that's not the way the law is. The law isn't sometimes in effect, and other times not. The law is constant—it is the same all the time for everybody.

We often hear, "Nobody is above the law". In essence, that means politicians, police officers, leaders, etc., will be held accountable if they break the law. It does not always work out that way, but that is the philosophy people desire to live by.

The same holds true in the spiritual realm. No exceptions. The Word doesn't work just for some people but not others. It's not that God likes only some people and causes His power to work for them. That's not it at all. God has established rules, and we need to learn how to abide in those parameters.

We can be confident that we will receive anything we ask, according to His will (1 John 5:14). How can we know God's will? God reveals His will in His word. "Beloved, I wish (will, want, desire) above all things that thou mayest prosper and be in health, even as thy soul prospereth" 3 John 1:2 (KJV).

God wants you to prosper and be healthy. God wants you to be a world overcomer. “Who is he that overcometh the world, but he that believeth that Jesus is the Son of God” 1 John 5:5 (KJV).

Press the Issue

If someone stole your car, you would have the right to press charges. You could demand the thief be picked up by the police and prosecuted. If he is found guilty, some kind of punishment, prison, or reimbursement can be assessed. Yet the thief’s disposition is all dependent upon the person who was wronged exercising her rights and pressing charges. In a sense, you have to take authority and say, “I am going to receive what is rightfully mine”.

This principle applies in the spiritual realm. Every believer has God-given rights and privileges. God has established His will for you, but it’s up to you to claim what God has done for you. You must press the issue. You must move in your authority to enforce those spiritual laws made for your benefit. Ignorance of these spiritual rules will keep you from “pressing charges”. When you operate as if you don’t have any authority or power, Satan interferes in your life at will. He will challenge you as he did Eve in the garden, or Jesus in the wilderness.

John 10:10 reveals both God's will and Satan's will quite clearly. "The thief comes only to steal and kill and destroy; I have come that they may have life, and have it to the full" (NIV).

Satan comes to steal, kill and destroy, but God comes to give you life more abundantly. If something in life is good, it's of God. But if an action is bad—stealing, killing, and destroying—it comes from the devil. Although this principle is a bit simplistic, it's true. Good God. Bad devil. Good things come from God and bad things come from the devil (James 1:17).

The Lord has ordained guidelines for your good so you can access the abundant life He has provided for you. You must learn these rules so you can follow them and demand Satan quit stealing, killing and destroying the blessings that are rightfully yours. Christians must be aware of our authority and God's principles in order to access all that He has promised to His children.

Ponder This:

(What, what would have become of me) had I not believed that I would see the Lord's goodness in the land of the living! Psalm 27: 13 (AMP)

What is the connection between knowing that God is good and trusting Him in your life?

____

____

____

Practical Practice:

Have there been times in your life when you did not know or believe that God is good? How were those times different from your periods of unquestioning trust in God?

____

____

____

Pray:

Dear Heavenly Father, thank you that you desire good things for us. Thank you that you have our best interests at heart because we are your children. Help us to align our thoughts with yours and see your goodness more and more in our lives. Amen.

CHAPTER 2

You Don't Know What You Don't Know

"But my God shall supply all your need according to ***his*** *riches in glory by Christ Jesus." Philippians 4:19 KJV*

With the memory of feeling squished into a small college desk, I can recall the light-bulb moment as if it were yesterday. I was pregnant but determined to finish the semester despite my growing girth. The professor was explaining a concept I knew nothing about and suddenly I felt cheated that no one had ever told me about these things called genetically modified organisms (GMOs). I was about to bring a baby into a world with such greedy industry that money trumped health and avarice undermined good. There was no unlearning this truth, and I somehow wished I didn't know the dangers of GMOs.

We live in states of being and knowing. There exists a state of total oblivion to things around us and can be described as the "don't know that you don't know" state. There is also the indifferent stage that claims, "I know but don't care because I don't think it affects me," state. And finally, the seeker stage presents a state of growth and stretching, where, "you know you don't know it all, yet pursue a better way". These apply to our spiritual life as well.

God is absolutely unlimited in His ability and His resources. And He is unlimited in His desire to pour out those resources upon us. Nothing delights Him more than the opportunity to give blessings from His abundance to His obedient children.

Wonderful, Heavenly rewards await you after you pass over. But God has vast earthly blessings ready for you to receive now in this life, as well.

Hebrews 1:14 calls us "heirs of salvation" as New Covenant believers. Most people think salvation simply provides them entrance into Heaven when they die. The full definition of the Greek word *soteria* specifies "deliverance, preservation, protection, material and temporal deliverance from danger and apprehension, pardon, protection, liberty, health, restoration, soundness and wholeness". Salvation includes everything you could ever need – whether eternal security or earthly matters. Deliverance includes healing for your body and provision for your family.

That is your inheritance! And it comes to you through faith in Jesus as the Lord of your life. Jesus is the perfect package of salvation through His life, death and resurrection.

Blessings Come Through Faith in Christ

"Even as Abraham believed God, and it was accounted to him for righteousness" (Galatians 3:6).

This verse from the New Testament takes us all the way back to Genesis. Paul uses the example of Abraham to tell us how God's blessing is received and enjoyed. Reflecting on the early part of Abraham's life, we see a great illustration of justification by faith.

The law did not justify Abraham because the Mosaic Law was not given until 400 years after Abraham's time. Neither can it be said that he was justified by the commandment of circumcision. Circumcision was the mark and evidence of Abraham's faith. God told Abraham that his seed would be as numerous as the sand on the seashore. God also told him to look toward the Heavens.

In effect, God said to Abraham, "You can't count the stars, and neither can you count your offspring." Do you know Abraham's response? "And he believed in the LORD; and he counted it to him for righteousness" (Genesis 15:6). The original language expresses that literally Abraham said "Amen" to the Lord. God said, "I'm going to do it". And Abraham said, "Amen".

But how does Abraham's story apply to our lives today and the blessings we long to receive? Well, God is looking for our "Amen", our agreement to the promises available through Jesus. God says to us, "I gave My Son to die for you. If you believe in Him you won't perish. You will have everlasting life".

Will you say "Amen" to that? Will you believe God? Will you accept His Son? If you do, you are justified by faith.

So God made all the promises, and the covenant depended on God's faithfulness. More than 2,000 years ago Jesus Christ went to the cross to pay for our sins. He completed the contract. He is the One who made the promise and the covenant, and He saved us.

Other translations of Galatians 3:6 use the word "accounted" and in Genesis 15:6 we see the term "counted". Both counted and accounted in these contexts mean the same as the word "imputed" in Romans 4:11, 22 - 24. The Greek word for imputed means "to put to one's account." When the sinner trusts Christ, God's righteousness is added to his account. More than this, the believer's sins are no longer put to his own account (Romans 4:1-8).

Inherited Salvation is Errant

Some people today still believe that salvation is inherited. Because Mom and Dad were godly people, the children assume they are automatically saved. But this is not true. "God has no grandchildren," as the saying declares.

God asks us individually to believe Him, to put our trust in Christ and be saved. What a magnificent picture of faith we have here. God wants your faith to rest on a solid foundation. But, my friend, if you come to God, you must come to Him by faith. When you and I trust Christ as Savior, we are saved the same way Abraham was saved—by faith.

God's Blessing a Central Theme of Scripture

In the beginning, when God created the world He blessed it. That doesn't mean that He just wished it well. God's blessing on something empowers it to fulfill His purposes.

God promised Abraham a family that would outnumber the stars, a land to call his own, and a blessing to empower him for life. The story of the Bible becomes the progressive development of that promised blessing. The blessing is the theme that runs through the whole Book and is fulfilled in Christ our Redeemer.

God's blessings have always been received by faith. Abraham's misdeeds and failures did not exclude him from God's blessing, just as his good deeds did not earn him God's blessing. God still works this way today with His children. His blessing has always been realized through faith.

So how can we receive God's blessings? Through our faith, which is our obedience to God. We must recognize that God's blessing can come ONLY through faith. Even the Old Testament taught that man was saved by faith. It does not say that anyone was saved by keeping the law. The heart of the Mosaic system was the sacrificial system, a system designed to show us our shortcomings and our need for a Savior (Galatians 3:15-22). The need for grace.

The law states, "Do and live!" but grace declares, "Believe and live!" Paul's own experience recorded in Philippians 3:1-10, as well as the history of Israel told in Romans 10:1-10, proves that righteousness earned through works can never save the sinner; only faith can do that. When you understand that the blessings of God's grace come only through faith in Christ, the knowledge humbles, but liberates as well, "For you have been called to live in freedom" Galatians 5:13a (NLT).

So how can we receive God's blessings? Only when God presents the blessing as a gift made possible through Jesus Christ. Take God at His Word and rest in His grace. A simple, yet not easy principle, nevertheless this is the way to blessing.

The word "redeem" means to set someone free by paying a price for his freedom. As a result of what Christ did for us, we are saved from the curse of judgment and receive the blessing of grace. When you receive Christ, you are not only redeemed from something, but you are also redeemed **for** something.

Is God's blessing, received through faith in Christ, the source of your strength? Is your heart softened, sweetened, and strengthened because you know that through faith in Christ you are blessed by God? We must know that only by Him are our blessings possible. Only through accepting the work of the Cross and the indwelling Holy Spirit in us can we receive His blessings. Then we will be able to recognize the work of God in our life.

Are you certain of the things above in your life? He has freed us from our sin, he has freed us from the law, and now he just asks us to trust Him and to obey Him. He even provides us the strength through the Holy Spirit to do what He asks.

Will you trust God in faith for His blessings in your life?

Ponder This:

"But as it is written, Eye hath not seen, nor ear heard, neither have entered into the heart of man, the things which God hath prepared for them that Love him."

1 Corinthians 2:9

In what ways do we limit God's blessings?

____

____

____

Practical Practice:

In light of God's promise to his heirs, let your imagination run wild. What would be the best thing you can imagine God doing or preparing explicitly for you?

____

____

____

Pray:

Dear God, thank you for your complete gift of Jesus. We accept Him as Lord of our lives and ask for Your guidance to simply receive all that you have promised to us by faith. We ask for forgiveness of our sins and pray that You empower us to live for You. Amen.

CHAPTER 3

Examine Your Beliefs

"For You are my hope, O Lord God, You are my trust from my youth and the source of my confidence. Upon You have I leaned and relied from birth; You are He Who took me from my mother's womb and You have been my benefactor from that day. My praise is continually of You." Psalm 71:5-6 AMP

I knew a woman who I felt had gotten the short end of the stick in life. When I first met her she had been recently diagnosed with cancer. Yet the first thing I noticed about her wasn't her bald head but her smile. I questioned her strength, promised to pray for her and quickly went about my life. A few months later a prayer request came in from the same woman to pray for her husband in whose brain doctors had just found a tumor. Cancer struck this family again, and our hearts anguished for them. We offered more fervent prayers, and he seemed to be better when another tragedy struck. Leukemia. Her six-year-old son. How could one family endure such heartbreak? Yet asking for prayer always seemed to be their first choice and our church family, eager to help, obliged.

A few weeks after her son's funeral, she buried her husband. She allowed us to peek into the strength that seemed unfathomable to most. She was sure of her husband's and son's eternal home and knew it was only a matter of time before she would join them. Strength? Yes. Faith? Absolutely. Fair? Depends on your definition.

There's a cliché said among Christians where one person will say, "God is good". Then, another person will say, "All the time. And all the time...." The first person responds back with "God is good".

There's truth in that. God is good all the time, and all the time God is good. As followers of Jesus, we believe that God is good. But sometimes we struggle to believe that God is good toward us. Many of us wrestle with the difference between knowing that God is good in our heads and believing that God is good in our hearts.

One thing that I've come to realize in this journey called life is that it's okay to be honest. I endeavor to become ferociously honest in my journey with Jesus. In the past I would put on a smile, pretend that all was well and just barrel through my struggles. I thought to be honest would make me too vulnerable. I was an impostor.

Far too many Christians live an impostor life. We know the right things to say and the right things to do, but we often tussle with questions and doubts. Heaven forbid we bring up these doubts, struggles and questions in church! We'd be looked down upon. In many churches questions are threatening, doubts are dangerous, and struggles mean you don't have enough faith. That judgment is one reason why we are afraid to be honest.

Questions, however, are revitalizing. God is okay with our struggles, and doubt is a part of our wrestling with our beliefs and coming to faith. Putting our trust in the goodness of God at all times, seasons and circumstances of life is fundamental to receiving the blessings He wants to generously bestow. Yet we struggle sometimes to believe that God is good in all areas of life.

Nothing is more crucial in life than what we believe about God. In fact, that belief is foundational to everything else about our lives.

If we believe things about God that aren't true, we lay a faulty foundation for our lives that will sooner or later crack. If we have wrong thinking about God, we will have wrong thinking about everything else. Because, you see, what we believe about God ultimately determines the way we live.

A person can have a skewed view of God for many reasons. Let's look at some major beliefs that need immediate adjusting.

Bad Things Happen to Good People

This concept is probably the biggest struggle people wrestle with in the arena of faith. It's the age-old question: If God is so good then why do bad things happen to good people, especially Christians? If God is so good, then why doesn't He stop bad things from happening?

Sometimes this is hard to get our minds around. It's caused numerous people to shipwreck their faith, get lost in doubt and struggle greatly with the goodness of God. The truth is we will never know the complete answer to this mystery. We all have a hard time reconciling the goodness of God with a world full of evil at some time or another. When tragedy strikes close to home, we battle even more with understanding the goodness of God when faced with our own dark valleys of pain, hurt, turmoil and grief.

One issue we need to look at is that God's definition of goodness and ours are different. Much like our children's definition of what is good for them and our definitions are different. God does not see sickness, pain and misery as good things. Although bad things happen, God's love is stable through our storms. He has our best interests in mind. He will work out all things for our good because that's how God works. He takes the bad and turns it into good. We don't always know how, when or where the good will come, but it does. He will work it out to our good.

Even though we don't completely understand why bad things happen to good people, we can be certain that

God is good! Circumstances might not always seem good to us, but God is always good…all the time.

Don't Believe the Lie

When bad things happen to good people, we are tempted to believe that God is not really good. If He were, He would have—"(fill in the blank)". Or if He really were good, He would not have—"(fill in the blank)".

Now, we might not consciously believe that God is not really good. Even if we feel it, we would never dare to say out loud, "God is not really good" because theologically, we know better. We know in our heads that God is good. But I believe that deep in many of our hearts is this lurking suspicion that: Yes, God might be good to everybody else, but God has not been good to me. This lie is at the core of much of our wrong thinking about God.

In Genesis chapter 1 we read about what God made and then see the description. Everything God made was good. Of course it was because it was a reflection of a good God. But when Satan wanted to tempt the woman to rebel against God, he planted in her mind the seed of doubt about God's goodness.

When turbulence comes into our lives—disappointment, pain, loss of loved ones, or dashed plans—Satan tempts us to wonder, "Is God really good? If He were, how could He have let this happen? How could He have let my husband abandon me? How could He have let me lose my job? How could He have let my parents treat me this way? Or, why would God have kept this good thing from me?"

When you look in this fallen world at the wars, famine, or natural disasters, these things are a reality. Satan uses these realities to try to put God in a negative light. How could a truly good God let the Holocaust take place or the destruction happen in Syria?

Counter the Lie with Truth

Once we doubt the goodness of God, we're going to find it hard to trust God. You can't trust a God who's not good. Now, how do we counter that lie in our minds and hearts? We replace the lies; we displace lies with the truth. The truth is that God is good. He is good. He is good whether or not His choices seem right to us, whether or not we feel it, whether or not it seems true, and whether or not He gives us everything we want.

Dr. Larry Crabb wrote a wonderful book called *Finding God*. He talks about the goodness of God. In his book Dr. Crabb discusses how we must call God good even when we suffer, simply because God is good. And when things are going well, we must call God good for reasons outside our direct blessings.

When you have a sick child and your child gets well, you say, "God is so good. He healed my child". Well, that's true. God is good. And He did heal your child. But can you still look up into the eyes of God when your eyes are filled with tears and your child doesn't get healed and say, "God is still good"? Our perspective is so limited. We cannot see and know what God sees and knows.

Burying a child is something no person should ever have to endure. Ever. But in life, we face seemingly insurmountable challenges, and the choice is set before us as to how these circumstances will define us. One of my most poignant memories involves a song my brother-in-law sang at my sixteen-month-old niece's funeral. Sounds of epic anguish were broken when at the most unexpected time he sang the chorus of, "God is so good,

God is so good. He's so good to me". I truly could not comprehend the courage of this father at the time.

In *Finding God*, Dr. Crabb encourages us to take a look at things from God's perspective. He imagines God saying, *If you look for evidence of My goodness in what you see around you and inside you, you will reach a extremely wrong conclusion. You will resolve that sometimes I am good, and sometimes I am not. But if you look for evidence of my goodness in the way things will be one day, if you are willing to believe that I am at work now to prepare for that day, and if you consider the meaning of My death—then you will realize that all the badness in the world can no more overcome My goodness than a child can out-wrestle a man.*

We often struggle with expressing a desperate longing to feel and know the love of God in our lives. We battle seasons of oppression and torment. We desire desperately to know the love of God for ourselves and to be deeply satisfied in a love relationship with our Savior, but how? Surely if God loved me and I meant so much to Him, I would feel loved and valued.

The Disconnect Between What We Know and How We Feel

The devil wants us to believe that God is bad and is withholding good things from us. He wants us to believe that God is out to get us for erring yet again. He wants us to believe that we are not worthy of anything good. All of these are lies.

Unfortunately, many of us have built our lives upon these lies, and we tend to see God as a harsh taskmaster instead of a loving Father. We believe the wicked lies of the enemy and it's given us a false image of a loving God who is good. God's goodness is never based upon my goodness or worthiness. He is good whether or not we are good. His kindness isn't based upon the deeds of men. It's based upon His character and nature. I am good enough for the goodness of God because I am the object of His affection. His love for me makes me good enough for His goodness.

But do we believe this? In our minds, we know we're supposed to believe that God does love us. But many feel there is a disconnect between what we know and what we feel to be true. Now, therein lies one of the problems: We tend to believe what we feel rather than what we know is true.

And so, as we look at our relationships—you might be living in a loveless marriage, you might be experiencing rejection from an ex- or grown children who never come home to visit or call. Perhaps you're single, with another birthday approaching, and not a suitor in sight—no possibility for marriage. Your feelings say, "Nobody loves me". And the implication is, "not even God".

When we allow a seed of a lie to be planted in our minds, we dwell on the lie until we ultimately believe it's true. And sooner or later our behavior will reflect what we really believe. We will end up in bondage, eating the fruit of bad seeds. Those little seeds that we allow to come into our minds—"Maybe God doesn't really love me"—ultimately will take root and grow to produce an incredible harvest of great damage.

Counter the False Image of God

Religions and legalism have painted an image of God that causes us to cower in fear of Him. We don't believe that He will be good to us until we have performed well for Him. It's called the "treadmill of performance". We believe that the harder we run after God, the more we sweat for God, and the more tired we get doing good things, God will eventually see our effort and reward us. Religion has painted a picture of God whereby it becomes all about our performance, behavior and pursuit of God. Religion says that we must get God's attention to get God's goodness.

This is not true. God came looking for us. God's kindness leads us to repentance. In essence, His goodness brings us to Himself. He was good to us before we even knew anything about Him. Our performance, behavior, or conduct does not release His goodness. Only His love for us releases His goodness toward us.

The truth is that God does love us. God loves you. Each and every one of us—whether or not we feel love and regardless of what we have done, where we have been, or what our past is. God loves us with an infinite love.

His love, unlike our natural human love, is not based on what we have done. It's not based on our worth; it's not based on our performance; it's not based on anything we could do to please Him or to gain His favor; it's not based on our worth. His love for us is based on the fact that He *is* love. He doesn't love us because we're lovable; He loves us because He is love. We do not deserve His love, and we could never earn his adoration, no matter how hard we try. Yet God loves us because love is what He is.

We counter lies with the truth. Our hearts are washed with the water of the Word of God. We renew our minds. When we doubt the love of God, when we feel unlovable as we are, we go back to the Word of God to renew our hearts.

The apostle Paul had come to experience for himself the love of God on the road to Damascus, and he never got over the wonder of what the love of God meant in his life. Paul wrote, "[5] And this hope will not lead to disappointment. For we know how dearly God loves us, because he has given us the Holy Spirit to fill our hearts with his love. [6] When we were utterly helpless, Christ came at just the right time and died for us sinners. [7] Now, most people would not be willing to die for an upright person, though someone might perhaps be willing to die for a person who is especially good. [8] But God showed his great love for us by sending Christ to die for us while we were still sinners" Romans

5:5-8 (NLT). “For I am convinced that neither death nor life, neither angels nor demons, neither the present nor the future, nor any powers, neither height nor depth, nor anything else in all creation, will be able to separate us from the love of God that is in Christ Jesus our Lord” Romans 8:38-39 (NIV).

We need to be determined to conquer the lies to trust the very goodness of a Father who loves us unconditionally.

God is good . . . all the time. And all the time . . . God is good!

Ponder This:

Do you struggle to believe that God is good? Why? What's your story?

____

____

____

Practical Practice:

The Lord bless you, and keep you; The Lord make His face shine on you, And be gracious to you; The Lord lift up His countenance on you, And give you peace. (Numbers 6:24-26 NASB)

How can we apply this blessing to our own lives?

____

____

____

Pray:

Lord, may we learn to rest in your love and goodness even when we can't see it, feel it or struggle to believe it. Please help us to be rooted and established in love, may we come to understand more fully, how wide, long, high and deep is the love of Christ, and to know this love that surpasses knowledge that we can be filled to the measure of all the fullness of God. Amen.

SECTION 2

The 3 **UNs** *that Block Blessings*

CHAPTER 4

UN-*Forgetful*

"Bear with each other and forgive one another if any of you has a grievance against someone. Forgive as the Lord forgave you." Colossians 3:13 NIV

I have not fought in a physical war. However I have had my share of spiritual battles. And in both instances, if you find yourself in the trenches unprepared for combat, you will get hurt. Gashes on your body or your soul leave scars that remain tender for a long time. The slightest of collisions with the affected area can release pain and memories that might seem relegated to the past.

Ministry is not glamorous. It can be a battle of

sorts. When your plans conflict with God's, or when people wield armory that was meant to defeat the common enemy (not each other), we can be left reeling and confused about what should have been. Man's agendas and politics play a major role in the church system yet were not a part of God's design for His bride. What remains in the aftermath of these conflicts are painful memories, unwanted bounty of war.

Each of us, at some point or another, will feel hurt by someone. The pain caused by someone close to us distresses us most. Pain from trusted individuals will hurt more and last longer than pain caused by strangers. Outsiders, however stinging their comments are, don't know intimate details and have never shared in our private afflictions and heartfelt desires. But trusted advisors know our weak spots, and when they stab us in the back, the agony can linger for a long time.

Practice True Forgiveness

Have you ever told someone you forgave them? Have you ever said to someone, "It's OKAY... I have forgiven you?" What did you mean by that?

The word "forgive" means to pardon one's trespasses. It means to excuse a person from the things done against you, to absolve from any punishment. Forgiveness means to renounce your anger at that person and not to hold the incident against him.

Have you ever considered the innumerable times we have done that very thing to God? Can you count the times you sinned, had a sinful thought or doubted God? And yet, as believers, we are friends of God. Imagine what life would be like if God still remembered our sins. However, Hebrews 10:17 states, "Then he says, 'I will never again remember their sins and lawless deeds'" (NLT). Thank God that He doesn't remind us of our sins every time we pray or worship. God wants us to have a relationship with Him where we don't feel embarrassed every time we are in His presence.

When our daughters were little, they certainly knew how to forget fast. They might have just been corrected or we said the dreaded word "NO", but they seemed to forget so fast. Within minutes they forgot the momentary tears of correction and came running to sit on my lap and ask me to play with them once again. I love what Jesus said in Matthew 18:3, "*I tell you the truth, unless you change and become like little children, you will never enter the kingdom of heaven" (NIV).*

Some say, "I will forgive but never forget." However, true forgiveness is putting it out of your mind and out of your heart.

Jesus asks us to forgive—to do away with, not to inflict punishment—seventy times seven (Matthew 18:22). You cannot talk about the forgiving part without talking about the "not-forgetting" part. The power lies in forgiving and forgetting the pain inflicted. In the Lord's prayer, you ask for forgiveness, but it is related to your forgiving others. "And forgive us our debts, as we forgive our debtors" Matthew 6:12 (KJV).

The phrase "forgive but don't forget" should be "forgive AND forget." If you continue to remember wrongdoings against you, you are letting those past trespasses, those past actions that you forgave, cause resentment in your heart. You are letting those past transgressions affect your relationship.

If you believe you have forgiven but are not forgetting the hurt, you have re-created the hurt all over again. Philippians 3:13-14 is a shining example of forgetting and moving forward. "Brethren, I count not myself to have apprehended: but this one thing I do, **forgetting** those things that are behind, and reaching forth onto those things which are before, I press toward the mark for the prize of the high calling of God in Christ Jesus"(KJV emphasis added).

To forget does not mean you will no longer remember. Your memory stays intact; but when the memory rises, the hurt and negative emotional response will not rise. Forgiveness dissolves the emotional attachment to the event in the wash of divine forgiveness.

True forgiveness is forgetfulness. Letting go. Emotional wounds you inflicted or received are healed. The memory of the event is simply that—a memory. In the forgiveness and love of the Holy Spirit you forget the discomfort, not the event.

Forgiveness Always Begins with You

A present hurt, or a past one, occurs once. When the memory of the incident rises and you emotionally respond, you managed to repeat, duplicate, and multiply the original hurt many times over. This intensifies the pain and suffering. This is why the same hurt can rise many times during our quiet times of reflection.

Each time this occurs, it is not the old original hurt, but rather one of the many hurts you have reproduced. The most important work with forgiveness is not to take back and re-create that which has been forgiven by responding with emotion. Once you have forgiven yourself or others, the painful, attached emotion no longer exists. Forgiveness is a necessary ingredient in the purification process.

Forgiveness presents you the power to release others and releases you from your own hurts inflicted through memory. It frees you to move on; it's a choice of loving or not. Forgiveness and loving are one. How can you have one without the other? Jesus gives you an obvious choice, and as usual, He expects you to make the necessary choice for your own wholeness.

In choice, you are the one who ultimately benefits. You are the one who receives the blessing, who is set free. You are the one whose trespasses are forgiven by making the choice to forgive, and in the process you also set others free.

Forgetting Unlocks Blessings

So what does forgetting past hurts have to do with being blessed? Actually, a lot. I learned this lesson after getting hurt by someone I looked up to for most of my life. This person was someone I highly regarded and respected immensely. I never questioned anything he said. But one day, he accused me of something I did not do. I was devastated that he thought so little of me, and the relationship was severed beyond repair. Despite multiple attempts to reconcile our friendship, each attempt brought disappointment and I was faced with a choice: Hold onto hurt, or release the pain to God. I held on, daily rehearsing the wrongdoings and allegations, and with each memory rose a swell of negative emotion. I was crushed; I thought about the pain daily for years until I studied the life of one of my Bible heroes, Joseph. And I learned an amazing lesson that has opened great doors of blessings in my life emotionally, spiritually, and financially.

Joseph understood how to be fruitful and claim his blessings in a time and in a land where he should have been a slave. He suffered deep pain because of what his brothers did to him. But Joseph understood that the path to blessings and fruitfulness was to forgive and forget. Although not an easy lesson, it is invaluable to our spiritual growth. Forgetting doesn't mean losing some of your memory. It simply means it's no longer constantly on your mind. You no longer remember the hurt every time you see the person or if the name comes up in conversation. You no longer hold a grudge against him.

Whether you know it or not, hurt caused by others builds walls in your life. Walls that block blessings of all kinds. Walls that stop you from smiling or laughing or enjoying the life you have. These walls even affect you at work and in how you raise your children. Our natural response, many times, is to try and knock these walls down. I personally had walls in my life caused by past hurts and difficult circumstances. I remember praying, "Why me? Why are these certain people in my life? Lord, can you knock them down? Can you remove them from my life? I know you can. Can you eliminate the walls from my life God?" I repeated this plea until I studied the lesson hidden in Joseph's story and began to realize, "What if the walls are part of God's plan in my life? What if without these walls I could not become the person of strength God intended for me to be?" I realized that I could be praying for the removal of my blessings instead of claiming these disguised blessings.

Joseph's father, Jacob, loved him more than he loved Joseph's brothers, and it was obvious. Joseph had dreams of being a mighty man. He imagined his parents and all his brothers would come and bow before him. Of course, this caused Joseph's brothers to be jealous and as a result, they hated him. The brothers sold Joseph to Egyptian travelers as a slave. Later, Joseph was accused falsely and thrown in jail. All his dreams seemed crushed.

I wonder sometimes what our response might be to Joseph's circumstances. What if our own siblings hated us enough to want to kill us and sell us into slavery simply because of the level of animosity and jealousy in their hearts toward us? Would we run away or shut down? Surely we would stop dreaming.

Still Joseph overcame adversity and saw from an eternal perspective that his opposition was used to save many lives. Jacob, as he approached death, even prophesied over Joseph saying that he was a fruitful vine near a spring whose branches climbed over a wall (Genesis 49:22).

Like us, Joseph faced a wall. What his brothers did to him was so painful. Joseph's wall kept growing, and his dreams faced a dead end with seemingly no way to be fulfilled for this slave in a foreign land. But at all times, Joseph kept the Lord first and kept on waiting for God's promises to be fulfilled. Joseph's branches kept reaching a greater height to overcome the wall. He was blessed for it. And his faithful climb over the wall blessed many.

Forget, Then Be Fruitful

The Lord blessed Joseph, and he became the second in command to Pharaoh in Egypt. The Lord also blessed him with two sons. Joseph's life illustrates that in order to be blessed; you must first forget what others did against you. Joseph also proved that he had learned this lesson in how he named his sons. Joseph named his firstborn Manasseh and said, "It is because God has made me **forget** all my trouble and all my father's household" Genesis 41:51 (NIV). Joseph was supposed to suffer in Egypt, but instead he became fruitful. Joseph named his second son Ephraim and said, "It is because God has made me fruitful in the land of my suffering" Genesis 41:52 (NIV). And all his dreams came true.

Do you see how the wall was an important part of Joseph's life? The Lord didn't knock the wall down. What happened, happened. But Joseph learned how to grow over the wall, and God used that wall to his benefit. Because the wall was behind him, that same wall that blocked blessings from his life was now blocking curses. The same wall that obstructed success was now impeding failures. The same wall that blocked God from his life was now hindering the devil.

Joseph knew that if he had not gone through troubles, he wouldn't have become a man of authority. The same lesson applies to us today. Past hurts need not destroy us. Instead, God can use them to make us into the people of authority He envisions. Use your past pain to propel you forward, and you will grasp previously unclaimed blessings.

The Lord has strategically put certain people in your life to make you better and stronger. There will be rough times and times when you want to quit along the way, but stay strong and grow over your walls. The Lord will give you the strength to persevere. And when you do get past the wall, you will realize that the reason you are stronger is because of some of the incidents that God allowed in your life. Some of Joseph's last words to his brothers in Genesis 50:20 (ESV) were, "You meant evil against me, but God meant **it** for good" (emphasis added). The "it" in Joseph's comment referred to the "evil" they did. What Joseph was saying is God didn't knock the wall and remove the evil. Instead, *God used the wall and the evil for my good*. God wants to do the same for you.

Forget Your Old Glory

When we believe we have reached the ceiling of achievement, we limit our limitless God. As long as we have breath in us, we must always sense that God still has blessings for us. If we stop growing, we will stop the flow of blessings in our lives.

Sometimes our past achievements hinder blessings. Can you imagine a high-school student who finishes her eleventh year with honors then drops out of school? It would be as if it were all in vain. No matter how smart she is, she cannot stop studying and focus only on her old achievements. She must continue to look forward and try to keep the momentum going. I'm afraid many of us look back to our journey with the Lord and feel this has been great and we don't have to serve any more. The

Lord wants to take us from glory to glory. Once again, yesterday's glory is not sufficient for today.

I once knew an older preacher whom God had used in miraculous ways in the past. This pastor had documented, as a reminder, all the miracles God had performed long ago in one notebook. He called the journal "The Miracles Book". One day this pastor felt that he had done a great job for the kingdom and decided to take a break and focus on his personal life. Every time a visitor came, he asked his son to get "The Miracles Book" so they could reminisce. The son dutifully got the book and the pastor read what the Lord had done in the past. The visitor left defeated, not receiving the encouragement or miracle he was seeking. Day after day, visitor after visitor, the pastor repeated this behavior until one day, the pastor asked his son, as usual, to go get "The Miracles Book". The son returned saying, "Dad, a rat must have eaten "The Miracles Book". I can't find it. Maybe God is trying to tell you something." The preacher was so focused on the past, he forgot today. What about today? What is God doing with you today? Is God finished with you? The apostle Paul said that he must forget the past and go forward. We need to do so even if the past was glorious. We read in the Old

Testament about the prophet Jonah who was content with his ministry in his town with his people. But the Lord had bigger plans for him. Jonah didn't want to leave his comfort zone, he didn't want to travel, and he didn't want to expand his territories. Jonah didn't realize that God had a bigger plan for his life. God wanted to let Jonah learn a higher lesson, to increase his passion and love of even sinners.

God sometimes wants us to forget the glorious past, because the glorious past is not good enough for an ever-Glorious God.

Forget Yesterday's Failures

Just as our past glory can hinder us from God's best, so can dwelling in past failures. Maybe our past negative experiences make us afraid to move forward to claim our blessings.

When we lived in Florida for seven years, we endured many hardships. From health failures, to financial crashes, to ministry burnout and even the near collapse of our marriage, if it could go wrong, it did. The financial and ministerial hardships were some of the hardest to recover from. Being wounded in these areas caused a poverty mentality to take root, and building bridges of trust with the faith community was a road we were not eager to pursue. When we moved from Florida, we felt that ministry was relegated to the distant past—something we *once* did. And home ownership was a remote memory, as well. But the Lord wasn't finished with us. God started to deal with us, and we were obedient to Him. We got involved again in ministry. Immediately after participating in local ministry, the Lord opened the blessings from all different angles, mainly financially. We again owned a home at a time when banks were saying no to everyone in our situation. Don't let your failures or your sins stop what God has for you. Claim your blessings. They are yours, and blessings are not dependent on a successful past.

The apostle Paul didn't have an impressive past. His record was blood stained and tarnished. Still, he stopped looking behind him and he moved forward. Thousands of years later, we are learning from his life. Even in today's world, many people refuse to give in to failures or what others think of them. Walt Disney was fired by a newspaper editor because, "He lacked imagination and had no good ideas". Steve Jobs, founder of Apple, was fired from his own company. If the world can use the simple biblical principle of forgetting past failures, shouldn't we do it even before they do?

Focus on the Purpose

Life is busy and sometimes we get too focused on our daily living. We don't focus on the real purpose. Sometimes we focus on the problem and not the solution or the reason behind the problem. Months and years can go by without our seeing and sensing the blessing of God on our lives.

When a bird is captive in a cage, all it seems to think about is how to escape, losing its melody of delight in the process. But when the bird is free, it can focus on its purpose, to build a nest and have a family, and share its beautiful song of joy. When we are captive in daily busyness, all we think about is how we can make ends meet. The Lord wants us to be freed from magnifying the problems and instead focus on the purpose.

Looking back to Joseph's life, if Joseph focused on the problem and kept thinking of what his brothers did to him, he would have starved to death with the rest of the world. But because Joseph was close to God, he was able to claim his blessings and save the known world from starvation.

Let us focus on purpose, let us discover why we failed in the past. Let us fix what was broken, confess our sins, forget past pain and glory. And claim our blessings.

We must believe that God has our unclaimed blessings waiting for us to grasp. God might consider our glorious past as training for the future as in Jonah's life. God can also use our painful past to save the world like He did with Joseph. No matter what our past was like, let's forget it and go forward toward what God has for us. The Lord is not finished with us yet and has many unclaimed blessings waiting.

Ponder This:

Has someone close to you ever hurt you? When you say you have forgiven someone, have you truly forgiven them? Are you saying it because it is true, or because you feel it is the right thing to say? Today, if there is someone you have not forgiven, if there is someone you are still angry with, take time to make it right (Matthew 5:23-24).

____

____

____

Practical Practice:

The power of forgiveness is given to you. Ours is the same power Jesus had when He walked on earth. The power God gave Him, He has given you. Realizing this, how could you choose to forgive and forget?

____

____

____

Pray:

Dear Lord, please help us examine ourselves. Help us to forgive and forget those we can't seem to release. Give us your grace to do your will. Amen.

CHAPTER 5

UN-*Grateful*

"I am not saying this because I am in need, for I have learned to be ***content*** *whatever the circumstances." Philippians 4:11 NIV*

Raising teenagers requires daily sanctification. I joke that raising our teenagers has kept me closer to Jesus than anything I have ever experienced. We have heard it all and experienced it all, from the, "But everyone has the latest..." to "You can't possibly understand what I am going through," to the frequent, "I hate my life" rants. Yes, the teenage years can be hormonally-charged tough times, but how often do we act like privileged juveniles with God?

Have you ever raised a teenager? Even if not, you have been one and can relate to the turbulent years of adolescence. Teens can be some of the most entitled and ungrateful creatures on earth as they wrangle their way into maturity.

Have you considered that if we take the time to thank God for everything He does for us, we wouldn't have time to complain about anything that goes wrong in our lives. We know that giving God the thanks He deserves is important, but in most cases, we really don't give him the appropriate appreciation or show Him how grateful we are. Is an ungrateful heart leading you to miss blessings? What about promises? Does our thankless attitude block God's promises from being fulfilled in our lives?

Recognize this, God takes care of us 24/7, He always does well for us. Even when things go wrong, He is still in control, and He has a plan to make good out of bad circumstances. Instead of receiving thanks from us, He receives complaints and ungrateful attitudes. What would you do if you generously helped someone continually and all you received in return was complaining and ungratefulness? Could our murmuring be slowing blessings from manifesting in our lives? In this chapter we will see how important thanksgiving is and how we need to be grateful all the time even during pain and suffering.

Not everything that happens in our lives feels good. We don't always feel like we should be appreciative. How could Paul suggest, "giving thanks always for all things to God the Father in the name of our Lord Jesus Christ" Ephesians 5:20 (ESV)? Was Paul trouble free? No. In fact, Paul suffered countless difficulties. Soon after he accepted Jesus Christ as his Lord and Savior, God told him what to expect in his lifetime. God revealed to Ananias what was about to happen to Saul/Paul. But the Lord said to him, "Go, for he is a chosen vessel of Mine to bear My name before Gentiles, kings, and the children of Israel. [16] For I will show him how many things he must suffer for My name's sake" Acts 9:15-16 (NKJV).

Yet Paul still wrote, "Who shall separate us from the love of Christ? Shall tribulation, or distress, or persecution, or famine, or nakedness, or peril, or sword?" (Romans 8:35 NKJV). This sounds like someone who has no idea what everyday real-life is like. But in reality Paul knew that he would face obstacles. Paul recounts some of his suffering in 2 Corinthians 11:23-28. He endured countless trials, imprisonment, and frequently faced death. Paul bore hundreds of lashes from the Jews, beatings, and stoning. Paul survived three shipwrecks. He faced danger in the waters and from robbers, Gentiles, and even his own countrymen. He faced threats in the city, wilderness, and even in the sea. Paul confronted hunger and thirst, sleepless nights in the cold, and nakedness. How could he be thankful at all times? He learned contentment.

Taking for Granted God's Goodness

No one likes to feel overlooked, especially when you have gone out of your way for someone, and then you are disregarded. I will admit little things get to me when I try to be polite and am met with thanklessness. For example, when I let a motorist in front of me and they don't acknowledge by waiving their hand "thank you". Or, when I hold the door for a few seconds for the person behind me and they don't acknowledge me. Or, if I help a drifter with loose change and they look up and down at me as if to say, "Is that all?" But I'm guilty of doing the same toward God. Do you thank God for everything He does for you? When we don't, we are simply taking for granted His goodness. Many times, we thank the Lord for a meal, but we feel we don't need to thank Him for *everything* we eat.

Have you ever wished you could take back a present from someone who didn't show appreciation? While our intention may not be to receive a thank you, some kind of gratitude is often anticipated. David knew that he might easily overlook the goodness of God so he sang in Psalm 103:2: "Bless the Lord oh my Soul, and forget not all His benefits." Many times we take for granted the daily benefits and mercies of God. And that's why David was telling his soul not to forget God's goodness. Our busy lives shouldn't make us neglect thanking God for *anything*. We need to follow David's example and always remind ourselves of God's goodness.

David mentioned four benefits that we easily forget. He reminded himself not to forget God's forgiveness. As we sin daily, God's forgiveness covers us. Yet, we often forget to thank Him daily for his forgiveness. David reminded himself not to forget God's healing. When you feel healthy every day, do you thank Him every day? The third blessing David reminded himself of was not to overlook his redemption. (*I'm redeemed from sins and I'm righteous in the eyes of God because of what Jesus did for me. Works no longer redeem me, thank God, because I can never work hard enough to redeem myself.*) Last, David wanted to continually remember that God crowned him with love and compassion. Do you feel you have been crowned by God's love?

An attitude of gratitude should become a daily habit for us all. Too often we miss blessings because we overlook and neglect what God has done and is doing in our lives. He crowns you with love and compassion daily. God deserves all the glory, all the honor, all the thanks, and all the praise, daily. Do we recognize this goodness daily?

Complaining and Grumbling

If we know God is good all the time and He is in control, why do we complain? We complain because we forget His goodness. Having a negative mindset toward the goodness of God causes us to lose sight of His goodness. Paul taught that we need to thank God for everything, the good or the bad, as God can use the bad for our benefit. Before we complain about anything that's not going our way, we need to stop and thank Him for everything good going our way.

Thousands of years ago God delivered His people from Pharaoh. The Israelites had seen the hand of God through many miracles. They had seen the Lord turn water to blood and then back to water again. They saw other children dying but not their own. They even saw God divide the sea and bring water out of a rock. Do you think that should be enough for them to understand that God has a plan and is in control? Yet, they complained continually. They whined and grumbled to the point that they preferred to go back to slavery in Egypt over freedom, living in miracles with God. They never received or entered the Promised Land because of their lack of faith and complaining against the Lord.

Job was another man who, to some of us, had valid reasons to complain and grumble. In one day, he lost everything he owned. What is worse is that same day he lost all ten of his children in a tragedy. His wife, frustrated with their circumstances, told Job to curse God and die. Life was not worth living anymore from her viewpoint. And many of us do just that. We complain, protest and move away from God as if He is the bad guy. The Bible tells us in all this Job never sinned or charged God foolishly. Job learned an important lesson by not complaining or grumbling against what God allowed. In the end, because Job sought to understand God's plan for his life, God returned twice all of Job's losses. In addition, the Lord gave him ten more children bringing his total offspring to twenty. Grumbling can hinder or delay blessings. But fully trusting God can allow His ways to unfold in your life.

The choice is ours today. We can be thankful all the time or we can complain. We shouldn't be surprised if friends and family hurt us and take away what's ours. Neither should we be surprised if things happen in the world that will hurt us. Our grateful attitude to the Lord will lead to receiving our unclaimed blessings. Our thanks will take our life from defeat to victory, from prison to freedom, from poverty to riches, and from hunger to fullness.

Coveting and Becoming Greedy

In the book of Exodus chapter 20, the Lord gave His people Ten Commandments to live by. Nine of those commandments seem to be a list of outward actions—to do or not to do —toward God or people. The tenth commandment states not to covet, and covet is an inner feeling inside us, not necessarily an outward action toward someone and shouldn't necessarily hurt anyone. But, would God put something unimportant in the Bible? Of course not, therefore we need to spend some time understanding covetousness.

Covetousness means you disagree with what God has given you. Coveting is another way of showing ingratitude. If we covet, we are simply demonstrating with our thoughts that God is unfair. Covetousness also indicates that our desires are on materialistic things and not looking at Heavenly or spiritual things.

But let's be honest with each other, we sometimes sense that what we have is discriminating, or that life in general is not fair. Sometimes we feel God has given someone else more money, a better job, or better spouse. But if we really rely on God and believe that He knows best and He knows our future, then we should be content with what and whom we have.

Covetousness denies the Lord as Jehovah Jireh, "the one who provides all my needs". Philippians 4:19 reads, "But my God shall supply all your needs according to His riches in glory by Christ Jesus" (KJV). So, if God will provide all our needs, why do we covet? We need to be careful, because if we covet, we might gain something worthless. But if we feel content that God will supply all our needs, we will see that He will give us beyond our imagination.

Covetousness is a hidden sin that can creep into our lives unrecognized. It often starts with a feeling or thought that blossoms and changes the course of our heart's desires. You might be living in covetousness and not even realize it. Jesus spoke about covetousness and greed in Luke chapter 12. A man asked Jesus to divide the inheritance with his brother. The parable of the rich fool was Jesus' reply to the man and to us. Jesus warns us against covetousness and greed.

I work with many people who spend a tremendous amount of hours on the job and hardly any time with their families. Spending time with God is not even something they would consider. Many of them choose to work longer hours for overtime, commission, or promotion. There is nothing wrong with working hard, but is it worth spending your life making money and spending less time on things that actually matter?

Once we stop focusing on what's wrong and start focusing on thanking and praising God, the blessings will start flowing, and we will begin to see His promises fulfilled.

Ponder This:

"Therefore do not be anxious, saying, 'What shall we eat?' or 'What shall we drink?' or 'What shall we wear?' … your heavenly Father knows that you need them all." Matthew 6:31-32 ESV

What is the connection between worry and covetousness? What does God promise regarding this?

____

____

____

Practical Practice:

What would you do if you generously helped someone continually and all you received was complaining and ungratefulness? Could our murmuring be slowing down blessings from manifesting in our lives? How can you begin to adjust your thinking and your actions toward this?

____

____

____

Pray:

Jesus, please help our hearts find contentment in you. Fill us with gratitude and help us to see your goodness in our everyday lives, we pray. Amen.

CHAPTER 6

UN-*Faithful*

"His master said to him, 'Well done, good and faithful slave. You were faithful with a few things, I will put you in charge of many things; enter into the joy of your master.'" Matthew 25:21

Recently for Mother's Day my youngest child gave me a precious gift. The "All About my Mom Book" came wrapped in pretty preschool scribble and adorned with precious handprints that will never again be that size. I truly love these kind if gifts; however, what was most striking to me was my daughter's description of her mother. The usual descriptions gushed throughout the book, but one question stuck out at me like a sore thumb. My child was asked what her mother does, and her reply puzzled me and resonated deeply all at once. She answered, "My mommy is a juggler." Now, to clarify, I have never once successfully thrown and caught balls successively in a circular pattern in the air. Never. But her reply resonated because I always *feel* like I am juggling. House. Career. Kids. Marriage. Ministry. Friends. Always juggling. And perhaps not always so well.

Are you a juggler, too?

Never have humans had so many options in which to invest ourselves. During the week, hundreds of things vie for our attention: work, family, school, meetings, church, TV, sports, friends, and 101 other recreational activities. The weekend is no less full. Likewise, Christians have never lived in a time when faithful commitment is more important to God's kingdom.

Even if we weed out the unproductive activities we find in our lives, we still have so many good things where we can invest ourselves. Serving on the school board or helping in a scouting program is not a bad thing. However, even good things, when they take away from our faithfulness to God, can damage our spiritual connectedness.

A missionary to Haiti told me that the greatest challenge she faced in her work was deciding how to best allocate her time. In the country she was serving, this missionary observed an infinite number of things she could do to help others and in turn share the gospel. However, she had to use discretion in determining what would be the most fruitful for her commitment.

We can give only four things in our service to the Lord: our time, talents, treasure, and trust. Only these things can we offer to God. Truthfully, they are not even ours to offer, only ours to offer back. A rift in our faithfulness in these areas can block blessings in our life.

We cheat God when we declare with our actions that we are too busy to be faithful. Therefore, we block our own access to His best for our lives.

When we begin to see that everything we have on this earth is a gift from God, our perception of faithfulness in these areas changes. The Bible says in James 1:17, "Every good and perfect gift is from above, coming down from the Father of the heavenly lights". So, birth and life itself is a gift from God. Food and harvest come from the Lord. Family comes from God. The gift of work and career comes from the Lord. Our church and its ministries come from the Lord. And all of our material possessions come from the Lord.

We are to be good stewards of the possessions and gifts God gives us. First Corinthians 4:2 tells us, "Now it is required that those who have been given a trust must prove faithful" (NIV).

Consider the distinction between a steward and an owner. An owner possesses, while a steward cares for something. A good steward is a responsible caretaker of God's blessings. Stewardship is really defined by the difference in how we look at our possessions. The Bible says in Ecclesiastes 5:15 (NLT), "We all come to the end of our lives as naked and empty-handed as on the day we were born. We can't take our riches with us". We will leave all of our earthly belongings here on earth when God calls us home. Shifting our mindset from owner to steward will help loosen the grip that sometimes binds us to possessions. Our possessions don't belong to us anyway.

Stewardship is simply a Christian's attitude that demonstrates to God: *Everything I have Lord, belongs to you. Use it as you see fit.*

While growing up, I heard an ancient Eastern story that illustrates this point well. The story tells of a rabbit that dug a hole in the middle of a large field. Being proud of his new home, the rabbit declared to his fellow forest mates, "This field belongs to me!". The ground hog at the other end of the field quickly scurried and rebutted, "No, this is my field". Next the stately deer walked through the field eating the grass and declared, "No, it is definitely my field". While the hawk that flies in the air and catches the mice in that same field said, "This is indeed my field". However, in a few years' time all of these animals will be gone from earth and their offspring will be saying the same thing, "This field belongs to me". To whom does it really belong?

Just like that field did not really belong to any of the animals, this world is not our home! We are just passing through. We are here only for a limited number of years, and then God will call us home into eternity. We are not owners; we are stewards of God's blessings in this life. And being faithful with our time, talents, treasure, and trust releases greater blessings to steward.

The Four T's of Faithfulness

Let's examine four aspects of being good stewards of God's blessings.

1. Time
2. Talents
3. Treasure
4. Trust

First, understand that all four need to go together. Time or talent without treasure is not adequate; treasure without trust is not enough. All four need to be a part of the life of the growing Christian.

Time

Faithfulness with our time is not a modern day dilemma. Mankind has always been tempted to spread ourselves too thin. Yet dedicating our limited hours that each day offers to God first will bring order and meaning to our lives. I can with full honesty say that giving God the first-fruits of my time has unequivocally changed the outcome of my days. And the days that duties and busyness crowd out my quiet time, everyone notices, most of all me.

Another way we can faithfully give of our time can be in how we bless others with it. Giving your time can help show love, encouragement, and more for other people. If you have free-time, purpose to use it to benefit the Kingdom of God. Giving our time in this selfless manner is not convenient and not always glamorous, but it is necessary for growth. Using our time wisely is another way to be faithful. When God gives us free time we should use it wisely. Do we go out of our way and bring food to the elderly or the shut-ins? Do we serve others in ways that we cannot tangibly receive anything in return? You can give your time in many ways to help benefit the Kingdom of God.

Galatians 2:20 says, "I have been crucified with Christ and I no longer live, but Christ lives in me. The life I now live in the body, I live by faith in the Son of God, who loved me and gave himself for me" (NIV). This verse helps us understand that as Christians, our lives do not belong to us. We have been crucified with Christ and our lives belong to Christ. Therefore, God's goals need to be our goals. The Lord's values need to be our values. Consequently, if Christ wants the church to grow, then we should give generously of our time, talents, and resources to achieve those goals.

I knew of a church that was faithful with giving the Lord's tithes, but members were short on time to volunteer to give time to the work of the Lord. The church outsourced and paid for all the things that volunteers would do in most churches. Sadly, what I saw happen was that church became a "job", and the people who gave the most had the most control. I believe they missed wonderful opportunities to exercise their faith with voluntarily giving their time and talents.

I have also seen the opposite in churches. Christians give much of their time to the work of the church, yet do not give of their financial treasure. Time must be partnered with talent, treasure, and trust. In other words, they might bake cookies for a church function, sing in the choir, volunteer to serve in children's church, or in other ways give of their time, but they don't give financially to the work of the church. Giving our time to the church should never be a substitute for giving financially to the work of the Lord.

To come to a fuller understanding of this concept, we must ask ourselves, "Where is my trust? Where is my personal trust in God?" If God will take care of the sparrows of the field, will God surely take care of us if we trust Him and are faithful? Yes, He will (Matthew 10:29-31).

Another often-overlooked way to spend our time is in prayer. The least of us can, and should, pray. God answers prayer and therefore, why shouldn't we constantly ask God to help our church reach the lost? People a stone's throw away from us are perishing because they have not heard the gospel. Some of them do not wish to hear. Some need softened hearts. This is why we pray. God can and does change hearts. If we ask Him to do so, He will respond.

We must pray for our community and ask God to make us effective in reaching those around us. Always include the leaders of our communities and country in prayer. Lift up the church and church leaders in prayer. The list is endless as to what we can pray for. Let us begin with one thing today. Consider writing out your prayers and recording them in a prayer journal. Then as you witness God answering those prayers record the answer and date. It will change your attitude about prayer when you observe God in action in such a tangible way.

Talents

When we use our talents to benefit the kingdom of God, our talents become a gift. Are you using the talents God gave you to benefit His Kingdom? Time and talents can go hand in hand. Our Savior blessed you with the talents, so make them useful. Use your talents for others.

Our talents can be an offering to the Lord. Romans 12:1 tells us, "I appeal to you therefore, brothers, by the mercies of God, to present your bodies as a living sacrifice, holy and acceptable to God, which is your spiritual worship" (ESV).

Our talents come in the form of what we can do with our bodies and minds to build up the church. The apostle Paul asked us in this passage of Romans to offer our bodies to the Lord as a holy sacrifice. In other words, our talents can and should be used for the Lord's glory.

Teaching, working with people, singing, playing instruments, and cooking can further God's purposes on earth. Skills in organization, building, administration, and leadership, as well as in the fields of medicine and technical and mechanical work are also God-given talents. You developed all of your strengths, skills, and talents over a lifetime, and all were given to you to fulfill God's will.

Luke 6:38 says, "Give, and it will be given to you. A good measure, pressed down, shaken together and running over, will be poured into your lap. For with the measure you use, it will be measured to you" (NIV). Offering the Lord our talents blesses others. In return, God blesses us with overflowing abundance. Notice that the verse also tells us that with the measure you use, it will be measured back to you. In other words, give generously and it will be given back generously, give grudgingly and receive grudgingly.

Talents must be partnered with time, treasure, and trust. As we discussed earlier, when these elements work together, the effect is exponential. Giving only our talents to Kingdom work should never be a substitute for other forms of giving. But harmoniously melding these components was what God envisioned when He established His church.

So how do we use our talents for the Lord? First, we should know where our talents lie and how we can best use them. Several websites offer spiritual gift tests. Everyone should find where their gifts lie. Some people have gifts of service and can help with a plumbing problem, a broken window, or even mowing the lawn. Others have teaching abilities. Some people hold a lot of biblical knowledge yet are hesitant to share their wisdom. Other people have the ability to work well with children while some are comfortable working with those living in nursing homes. People with musical abilities can serve God through song. Other people are gifted in evangelizing. Seek God to help you discover and equip you better to serve Him and others with your talent.

Treasure

Malachi 3:10 says, "Bring the whole tithe into the storehouse, that there may be food in my house. Test me in this," says the LORD Almighty, "and see if I will not throw open the floodgates of heaven and pour out so much blessing that you will not have room enough for it" (NIV). This verse clearly defines and establishes the tithe or ten percent. More importantly, paying tithes acknowledges and communicates to God through our giving that He is the source. We honor Him by giving to His purposes. Giving also demonstrates that material wealth does not control us.

Tithing is not something we do to clear our conscience. It is not something that we do to so we can do whatever we want with the ninety percent that is left—it also belongs to God! We must seek His direction and guidance for whatever we do with the full amount. In seeking God for our finances, we may discover that God has different ideas than we do.

Everything you have gathered here on this earth will stay behind. So while we are here, becoming good stewards of

God's blessings is essential.

A kind older farmer loved the Lord and was a faithful Christian. He was a good steward of his property, finances, and all he owned. The farmer saw all of life as a blessing from God and gave to the church generously. He loved to tithe his money to the church and watch God work in many different ways through his gifts. God's faithful servant knew people were growing in their faith and his community was a better place as a result of his financial gifts. The farmer developed a plan to save money in a bank account large enough that when he died, his estate would provide an endowment for his church. The church was instructed to only spend the interest off of the principle from the funds, which would end up being the same amount he was giving as a tithe while he was alive. His plan was to continue tithing what God had blessed him with long after he died and remain doing so for hundreds of years.

The Bible tells us to be generous with our treasure as a part of our gifts back to the Lord. In the Old Testament when the people were to bring in grain or meat, the currency of the day, for their tithe to the Levite tribe. Over the past 4,000 years, we have moved from farmers and land owners to a variety of different careers, with money as the means to pay bills rather than produce or animals.

How we spend our treasure, or resources, matters to God,

not because He needs our treasure, but because we demonstrate where our trust and love abide.

Trust

Psalm 20:7 tells us, "Some trust in chariots and some in horses, but we trust in the name of the LORD our God" (NIV). Perhaps today this scripture could read, "Some trust in the wallet, credit card, and possessions, but a few trust in the name of the Lord our God".

Throughout the Bible the word trust comes into play. The very act and understanding of having faith in God is a matter of trust. Do you trust God?

When push comes to shove, you have to ask yourself the big question: *If I trust God, will He take care of me and my family to meet our needs?*

Philippians 4:19 answers that question. "And my God shall supply all your need according to His riches in glory by Christ Jesus" (NKJV).

There was a time in my life when the issue of trust was pushed to the limit. I can recall not knowing where our next meal would come from. Every ring of the phone brought worry and a pit in my stomach, for fear of another debt collector. Yet, I can also remember the feeling of unshakable trust that no matter what happened, our family belonged to God first. And more than our needs being our responsibility we knew He was responsible for us. We always gave our tithe. We could not waiver in giving back to God. We believed strongly that only God was our source and He always came through.

Trusting God was difficult at first, but whenever money appeared short, miracles occurred. As our trust grew, we witnessed more and more miracles—gifts, refunds, checks, bonuses. The way the finances came in was never the focus. Our awareness was always that we were blessed to witness His miracles daily.

God seemed to meet our needs, whatever they were. Things worked out. We became believers of God's care.

God's statement in Malachi 3:10 is not simply empty words. They are promises. God said, "I will open the windows of heaven for you. I will pour out a blessing so great you won't have enough room to take it in!" God said to test Him and see if he will not stay true to His word. Do you believe God would lie? Will He not bless you unimaginably if only you give Him what he asks of you?

If we are faithful in giving to the Lord through our time, talents, treasure, and trust, He will be faithful in blessing us so that we can be even better able to serve Him.

Ponder This:

What are ways that you can share your time, talents, treasure and trust for the service of the Lord? By being faithful in these areas how do you feel He has blessed you as well?

____

____

____

Practical Practice:

Are you vibrant, strong, and using your time, talents, treasure, and trust the way the Lord would have you? Or have you been lacking in your commitment? Have you been giving sacrificially to the Lord? Have you been using your time wisely and your talents for the service of the Lord? In what areas could you improve?

____

____

____

Pray:

Heavenly Father, help us to be faithful and be both a gracious and generous people with the blessings you have bestowed upon us. Allow us to see ourselves as good stewards rather than owners of what you have given us. Amen.

SECTION 3

Living it Out

CHAPTER 7

Ask, Seek, Knock

"Ask and it will be given to you; seek and you will find; knock and the door will be opened to you." Matthew 7:7 NIV

I heard a story of a man (Let's call him Bob), who some years ago found a wallet while walking down a street. Being an honest man, he wanted to return the wallet to its owner. So Bob opened it to look for identification. The wallet contained a few dollars, no driver's license and no pictures; nothing indicated who owned the billfold.

The young man looked through the wallet some

more and found an old envelope. It was wrinkled and looked as if it had been carried for years. The only part of the writing on the envelope that he could read was the return address.

To find more information, Bob opened the envelope. To his surprise, the letter was dated June, 1924. It had been carried in that wallet for decades. It was a “Dear John” letter written to a man named Joseph, and it was from a woman named Rose.

Rose explained that though she loved Joseph, and she would always love him, her parents had forbidden her to see him anymore.

Bob wanted to locate the owner of the lost wallet. He drove to the location listed on the return address. He parked the car and walked up to the entrance. A woman answered the door. He asked the lady if she knew a Joseph or a Rose. She told Bob that thirty years ago, she had purchased the house from a family whose daughter was named Rose. She said that Rose had placed her mother in a nursing home just a few blocks down the street.

Bob drove down to the nursing home and

explained the story to the nursing supervisor. She told him that the lady he was trying to find had died. However, she gave him a telephone number where he might locate Rose.

Bob learned that Rose was not living there anymore. The person who answered the phone said Rose was now in an apartment house for the elderly.

The young man began to wonder why he was making such a big deal out of an old, lost wallet that contained only a few bucks and a crumpled old letter. But Bob decided to persevere.

He finally tracked down Rose and went to visit her at the apartment house. She had an apartment on the third floor. Bob knocked, and a gray-haired, alert, bright-eyed lady with a warm smile answered the door. Yes, she was Rose Marshall.

Bob told her about finding the wallet and, showing her the letter, asked if she knew someone named Joseph.

Rose took the letter. Tears filled her eyes. She told him that the letter was the last contact she had with Joseph. She said that she had never married because she never met anyone she loved as much as Joseph. Then she asked if, when he found Joseph, he would tell him she still loved him and that she thought about him every day.

Intrigued but bewildered as to what to do next, Bob thanked her and left. As he walked down the apartment house hallway, he carried the wallet in his hand. The janitor saw the wallet and stopped him. "Let me see that wallet."

Bob handed it to him. "Why, that's Mr. Goldstein's wallet. I'd know it anywhere. He's always losing it." Bob asked where he could find Mr. Goldstein. The janitor said he lived in Apartment 6 on the 8th Floor.

So, Bob quickly made his way to the eighth floor. He found Apartment 6 and knocked. Sure enough, an old man named Joseph answered the door. He showed the wallet to Joseph. Bob asked Joseph if the wallet was his. Yes, it was. Bob admitted reading the letter to seek identification of the owner.

Mr. Goldstein asked, "You read it?" Then he told Bob that his life nearly ended many years ago when he lost Rose. He had never married and had never stopped loving her.

Then Bob beamed, “Mr. Goldstein, I think I know where Rose is”. The old man became very excited. Bob simply took him by the hand, led him to the elevator and down to the third floor to Rose Marshall’s apartment.

When she opened the door, they looked at each other in disbelief. Joseph Goldstein walked slowly to Rose. He took her in his arms. The sixty-year separation evaporated in the warmth of their love.

About three weeks after Joseph and Rose were reunited, Bob got a call asking him to be their best man. They were to be married after years of separation.

A 79-year-old man and a 76-year-old woman acting like teenagers must have been some sight! A perfect ending to a tragic separation. The couple had every reason to celebrate.

What if Bob had stopped or failed to follow through with his pursuit? The wallet was rightfully Mr. Goldstein’s, but he had no access to it. Had it not been for persistence, we would have missed out on a beautiful story of redemption.

"Ask and it will be given to you; seek and you will find; knock and the door will be opened to you" (Matthew 7:7 NIV). Ask! Seek! Knock! Cease not asking until you receive, cease not seeking until you find, cease not knocking until the door is opened unto you.

These two sentences seem to be a progression. The same thought takes another shape and becomes more persuasive. *Ask*—that is, in the quiet of your spirit, speak with God concerning your need. This is a good and acceptable form of prayer. If, however, asking doesn't appear to succeed, the Lord invites you to a more concentrated and active form of communication. *Seek*—actively let your desires complement your knowledge, thought, consideration, meditation, and practical action and learn to *seek* for the blessings you desire as people seek for hidden treasures. These good things are laid up for us, and they are accessible to fervent seekers. Seeking is the act of adding to asking—the study of the promises of God, a diligent hearing of His word, a meditation upon the way of salvation, and all other means of grace as may bring you the blessing.

Advance from asking to seeking; progress

toward it. And if after all it should still seem that you have not obtained your desire, then *knock*. Use not only your voice, but your whole soul. Diligently seek after that which you are praying. God often gives to His people when they keep His instructions that which He denies to them if they walk carelessly. Remember the words of the Lord Jesus, how He said, "If you abide in Me, and My words abide in you, you shall ask what you will, and it shall be done unto you." Holiness is essential to power in prayer, the lips ask while the heart seeks and the life knocks.

Ask for everything you need, whatever it might be. If what you ask is a right and good thing, it is promised to the sincere asker. Seek for what you have lost, for what Adam lost by the Fall, for what you have lost yourself by your neglect, by your backsliding, or by your lack of prayer. Seek until you find the grace you need.

Then knock. If you seem shut out from comfort, knowledge, hope, God, and heaven, then knock. For the Lord will open unto you. Here you need the Lord's own interference. You can ask and receive, you can seek and find, but you cannot knock and open—the Lord must open the door Himself or you are shut out. God is ready to open the door. The Lord Jesus Himself opens, and no man shuts.

It is about **a**sking, **s**eeking and **k**nocking, in short **A.S.K.**

Some people think they need to pray daily or constantly to God, while others believe they don't need to pray at all because God knows the future and they feel that God will do what He wants regardless of their prayers. Still others believe that God knows their needs without them asking. So why pray? Does prayer really do anything? Does it release blessings? If the Lord would ask us to pray without ceasing (1 Thessalonians 5:17), then it must be very important and can make a big difference in how our lives unfold.

Loving the Lord without spending purposeful time with Him is not enough. Mary and Martha in the Bible both loved Jesus, but one of them was busy and occupied with daily duties, while the other was intentional about sitting at His feet. Jesus commended the latter. Prayer is a daily decision. When we forgo communication with the Lord, our lives reflect the disconnect. In Psalm 23 David said of the Lord, "He leads me besides the still waters". But when David was in a season of being disconnected from the Lord, he said in Psalm 63, “My soul thirsts for you”. What a difference in the prophet after God’s own heart.

We pray that through this chapter you start to see the significance of daily connection with God. Sometimes we need to separate ourselves from what slows us from praying. Jesus did the same exact thing. He used to send the disciples somewhere so He could pray alone. In order to live the Christian life God has specially designed for each of us, we must make time alone with God a priority, even if that means temporarily separating ourselves from those closest to us.

The right prayers can be used to cash out our blessings and the wrong prayers delay or stop blessings all together. The right prayers play three important roles in claiming our blessings. First, they release blessings that are waiting for us to ask, seek, and knock. Second, prayers can take back what was stolen from us, and third, prayer helps fight evil spirits that want to stop our prayer from being answered. The wrong prayers on the other hand build partition walls between us and God that stops many things. Blessings are one of them.

Sometimes we don’t claim blessings because we

are not in God's will. Even though prayers don't change God's mind, they do allow God to change us and align us with His will. And God's will is always good.

Persistant Prayer

Ephesians 6:18 tells us to "Keep alert with all perseverance, making supplication for all the saints." A quality of Christian character, this verse illustrates the fruit of the Holy Spirit's work in our lives. Perseverance is a word most frequently applied in the face of opposition or trials. Perseverance is also often applied to how we should pray.

Jesus leaves no doubt that He is focusing on the subject of perseverance in prayer toward the end of the Sermon on the Mount in Matthew 7:7-11. Literally translated, the verse reads, "Keep on asking and it will be given to you; keep on seeking and you will find; keep on knocking and it will be opened to you" (v. 7). All three verbs are present imperatives, and likely, they are much more than just a repetition of the same idea. Rather, three commands "ask", "seek", and "knock" are a progressive amplification. Repeatedly asking requires perseverance, and still more so does continuous seeking. Persistent knocking suggests an intense desire for entry.

Luke in his gospel places in Jesus's teaching the parable of the persistent friend who comes to the door at midnight and refuses to be put off in his request for bread. "Because of his persistence" is Jesus's explanation of why the man obtains a response. But look more closely at each of Jesus's key words in this paragraph: "ask", "seek", and "knock" (Luke 11:5-13).

Asking is the most common plea in appealing before God's throne. One who is yearning for what he most needs, but knows who can supply his need uses this language. This language is of a child who has a need that his Father alone can satisfy. We are always safe when asking our Daddy God.

In the instructive verse of Matthew 7:9, Jesus draws a parallel with the experience of an earthly father-son relationship, "Or which one of you, if his son asks him for bread, will give him a stone?" The father delights to give good gifts to his son—not just any gifts, but good gifts. The son exercises familial faith in asking, and the father exhibits grace in giving.

Grace and faith are key fundamentals in prayer. In the case of our Heavenly Father's gifts, His perfect giving takes us into a new realm. The Father's gifts are perfect; that is why we should be so eager to come to Him.

If you wonder why God needs us to ask before He gives, remember two things. One is that He daily gives us good things we have not even thought about, much less asked for; the other is that in Psalm 2, we have a remarkable excerpt from a conversation between God the Father and God the Son regarding how the Son will have the nations for His inheritance and the ends of the earth for His possession. The Father says, "*Ask* of me, and I will give you" (Psalm 2:8). If the only begotten Son is told to ask, the children of God adopted by grace into His family should not be surprised that they too must ask.

Seeking reveals something more of God's character to us. God responds to those who seek Him (remembering, of course, that no one can truly seek God unless God draws him). And a seeker's heart is what gets God's attention. Seek Him, and choose to be chosen.

We need to listen to the emphasis on this in Jeremiah 29:13. God says, "You will seek me and find me, when you seek me with all your heart". God desires relationship with His creation.

Knocking is another escalation of asking and seeking. Perhaps the thought behind this word is earnestness. The man in Jesus's story who came to his friend at midnight displayed his seriousness in determined, persistent knocking. God responds to sincere persistence. Superficial supporters and spiritual entertainers will not engage His heart and mind.

So, when you pray, be a petitioner as a beggar, be a seeker as a child, and be a persistent knocker as a friend. True prayer demands all three.

Embrace the Space

What happens when we feel as though we have already persisted in ask, seek, and knock mode and are still living in lack? Philippians 3:12 tells us, "Not that I have already obtained all this, or have already arrived at my goal, but I press on to take hold of that for which Christ Jesus took hold of me" (NIV). This verse masterfully explains the answer. There is a journey between the brink and the blessing. There is a process between the place you are and the promise you've been assured.

Jesus Himself gave us a shining example of embracing the space in his wilderness experience for forty days. And even more amazing, He gave us a framework for what to expect after our own wilderness experience. Luke 4:1-15 details this account, "Jesus, full of the Holy Spirit, left the Jordan and was led by the Spirit into the wilderness, where for forty days he was tempted by the devil. He ate nothing during those days, and at the end of them he was hungry.

The devil said to him, "If you are the Son of God, tell this stone to become bread." Jesus answered, "It is written: 'Man shall not live on bread alone.'"

The devil led Jesus up to a high place and showed him in an instant all the kingdoms of the world. And Satan said to him, "I will give you all their authority and splendor; it has been given to me, and I can give it to anyone I want to. If you worship me, it will all be yours."

Jesus answered, "It is written: 'Worship the Lord your God and serve him only.' "

The devil led him to Jerusalem and had him stand

on the highest point of the temple. "If you are the Son of God," he said, "throw yourself down from here. For it is written: 'He will command his angels concerning you to guard you carefully; they will lift you up in their hands, so that you will not strike your foot against a stone.'"

Jesus answered, "It is said: 'Do not put the Lord your God to the test'". When the devil had finished all this tempting, Satan left him until an opportune time. Jesus returned to Galilee in the power of the Spirit, and news about him spread through the whole countryside. He was teaching in their synagogues, and everyone praised him" (NIV).

Four key points can be observed from Jesus's journey of temptation.

Key #1: Jesus was filled with the Spirit (v. 1). Jesus went into this wildnerness experience already filled with the Spirit. When we are filled with the Spirit, our hearts have no room for anything else. So get filled up. The Spirit sustains us for the trip.

Key #2: Jesus was led by the Spirit (v. 1). For us to be led by the Holy Spirit should be supernaturally natural. It shouldn't be weird or unfamiliar but rather a quiet assurance that He is leading.

Think of this leading as traveling in our cars with a GPS system with the voice guidance turned off. The GPS is still in our car, but we can't hear its guidance. We tend to ignore that guidance especially if we've turned off the voice.

Proverbs 14:12 tells us "There is a way that seems right to a man, but its end is the way to death" (ESV). Our own plans seem to be what is right for us, but truthfully if our plans are not submitted to His ways, then they lead to destruction. Leave the "what", "where", and "how" to the Spirit's leading.

Key #3: Jesus was separated. He was alone in this wilderness experience. Maybe, you too have felt alone in your wilderness? Isolated in the wilderness of sickness? Or was it perhaps the wilderness of debt? The good news here is that the wilderness experience was not designed to defeat us. It was designed to distinctly point out areas in our lives that need adjusting. In order for God to richly bless us, our character has to align with His calling. And the bigger the destiny, the bigger character is required.

The wilderness is not fun, but it is necessary. Getting frustrated in the process only delays the blessing further. Distraction brings delay. Eliminate distractions that delay distinction. What will you do in the wilderness? Wilderness is meant to draw us closer to God and separate us unto God.

Key #4: Jesus endured. Being tempted for forty days tests what you are made of. During the wilderness we are asked, "Are we going to trust God to take us through the space between?" The temptation will not be more than you can bear, no matter how hard it gets. "No temptation has overtaken you except what is common to mankind. And God is faithful; he will not let you be tempted beyond what you can bear. But when you are tempted, he will also provide a way out so that you can endure it" 1 Corinthians 10:13 (NIV). Stand firm on His promises.

So Ask, Seek, Knock, and embrace the space of the journey to your best blessed life.

Ponder This:

What are some things you might need to ask, seek, and knock about? In what areas have you persisted and seen God respond?

____

____

____

Practical Practice:

Have you faced "wilderness" experiences in your life? What can you take away from looking at the "wilderness" differently?

____

____

____

Pray:

Lord Jesus, please help us to seek you and know your love toward us. Draw us near to you and help us persevere. Thank you for the wilderness experience and help us to come out with deeper understanding of Your goodness. Amen.

CHAPTER 8

Act As If

"Therefore I tell you, whatever you ask for in prayer, believe that you have received it, and it will be yours."
Mark 11:24 NIV

With my knees knocking, I exited my car to meet my first client. A crisp new suit and shoes that were not yet broken-in bespoke my profession better than my sweaty hands. I had my license and passed the real estate exam with a near-perfect score, but I still felt so unprepared. A forced smile hid the fear in my voice, and I pretended to know what I was doing. Over time, this exchange became more comfortable, and I grew into the agent I once longed to depict, but those first few fearful client introductions are etched in my memory as an unlikely lesson in faith.

What do you need from the Lord? Healing? Prosperity? Finances? **The truth is, the Lord has already done His part. Many times we don't have our prayers answered because we have yet to perceive it.**

You might be thinking, *but I've got a doctor's report to prove I don't have healing* or *you haven't seen my bank account*. Regardless of what the natural details are, the truth is that God has already given you whatever you need. Second Peter 1:3 says, "According as his divine power hath given unto us all things that pertain unto life and godliness, through the knowledge of him that hath called us to glory and virtue".

The Thing Lacking is Knowledge

Scripture tells us that God *has already* blessed us, already forgiven us, already favored us, already approved and accepted each one of us. He is not waiting to do it; God already did these things. As far as God is concerned, the blessings with your name on them already belong to you. The real question is, "When are you going to go get what's yours?" God said yes to you being blessed, yes to you living healthy and whole. Yes to you accomplishing your dreams. Why don't we have the boldness to go get what already belongs to us? What if we believed our Heavenly Father loved us so much that we had the confidence to pursue what already belongs to us? Favor with your name on it belongs to you. It is already yours.

Whose Approval?

Some people live their entire lives trying to gain approval so they can feel good about themselves; they think if they work hard enough, have enough success, move into the right neighborhood, or convince a certain person to like them, then they will be happy. The good news is, you've already been approved. Jeremiah 1:5 tells us, "Before I formed you in the womb I knew [and] approved of you" (AMP). We often get caught up in trying to work for something we already have. The approval you earn or feel has nothing to do with whether you are good enough, lose twenty pounds, or have the right friends. No, God has already approved you. When God created you, just like He did with Jeremiah, He looked at you and said, "That was good; another masterpiece". Don't live intimidated and insecure, trying to earn people's approval. You have Almighty God's approval. There is freedom in this understanding.

Paul wrote, “Praise be to the God and Father of our Lord Jesus Christ, who has blessed us in the heavenly realms with every spiritual blessing in Christ” (Ephesians 1:3 NIV). Paul declared that God **has** already blessed. He’s not thinking about blessing you; He’s already shown you favor. You might not *feel* blessed, and your circumstances might appear otherwise, but the truth is He has blessed us. It might be easier to think, “When I see it, I’ll believe it”. But faith is the opposite. You must first believe, and then you will see in the way the Sovereign Lord wants to reveal His blessings to you.

Instead of talking about how bad your situation is, start declaring, “I am blessed. I am prosperous. I am the head and not the tail. I lend and I don’t have to borrow”. In order to start walking in the blessings, you have to talk as if you’re blessed, think like you’re blessed, walk like you’re blessed, act like you’re blessed, live like you’re blessed. Believing and acting in faith is what **activates** the blessing. Stop reacting from a limited mentality. When somebody asks how you are, instead of responding, “I’m just hanging in there. It’s really, really bad,” begin to represent yourself as the blessed child of the Most High that you are. Notify your face, put a smile on, hold your head high, and walk with confidence. You're a child of God Almighty, you have royalty in your blood, and you were created to reign in life.

Change your positioning

The price has been paid for your abundance, health, victory, and dreams. Through Jesus's sacrifice, it was finished. You've got to do your part and go get what's yours.

I am directionally challenged. It is a fact. It's actually remarkable that I don't confuse my right from my left hand half the time, so needless to say, I frequently rely on my GPS. One time I recall being lost in a mountainous, unfamiliar (aren't they all?) area and not being able to get the signal I needed for guidance. My GPS kept placing me on unmarked obscure areas that were not even on the map and clearly not where I was. The positioning of the system was off, therefore I could not get where I needed.

This happens with our lives as well. You might say, "I've been praying for favor. I've been asking God to bless me." Here's a key: Reposition your prayers. I sometimes don't feel equipped to minister, but I know that God already anointed and equipped us. So I've learned to shift my supplications from, "God, please give me your anointing," to, "Lord, thank you that I am anointed. Thank you that I am well able." You might not feel blessed, confident, strong or talented, but don't fall into that trap and go through life with a "poor old me" mentality; Get in agreement with God. He says you are blessed, you are strong, you are talented, you are victorious. He's already made you more than a conqueror. He's already crowned you with that favor.

You Already Have *All* Spiritual Blessings

Because you already have all spiritual blessings, asking God to bless you or waiting for Him to bless you is counterproductive. Yet many Christians start from that position. If they're sick in their bodies, instead of starting from "by His stripes, I *was* healed" (1 Peter 2:24) or "I have the same power that raised Jesus from the dead living in me" (Ephesians 1:19-20), they'll take the doctor's report or the pain in their bodies and say, "I'm sick. God, will You heal me?" They start moving *toward* victory instead of coming *from* victory!

One time, I was praying for healing for my daughter, who was little at the time. I wasn't seeing her healed, so I began to question God and felt frustrated in the process. I felt the Lord speak to my heart, "*You're fighting to get your daughter healed instead of understanding she is healed.*"

What is the difference? Instead of defending my daughter's healing and releasing what Jesus already provided, I was begging Him to do something He had already done.

Our misconceptions about this concept can be a chief reason why we feel we are not receiving from God. This needs to be a tangible revelation and must be followed by a change of thinking. Jesus already provided everything you will ever need. You're blessed with all spiritual blessings—all of them!

God moves in the spiritual realm (John 4:24). Whether we see a physical manifestation of what He has done in the spiritual realm is dependent upon what we believe and how we act, not on what He has done. It's not up to the Lord to heal us; He's already healed us (1 Peter 2:24). But He gave His miraculous power to us to release.

Healing has already been provided. Financial prosperity has already been provided. Joy and peace and everything that you will ever need emotionally have already been provided. If you're having a down day, if things aren't going right, if you don't feel good, you don't need to embrace discouragement, despair, and hopelessness. And yet we revert to this way of praying first, saying things such as, "Oh God, I ask You to touch me. I ask You to give me joy." The Bible says you've already received all these things. The logical question to ask, then, is "Well, where are these blessings?"

In Galatians 5:22-23, Paul says love, joy, peace, longsuffering, gentleness, goodness, faithfulness, meekness, and temperance are in you if you're born again. These things are imparted to you as a believer.

God loves you whether you feel it or not! His love has been poured in your heart—in other words, in your spirit. And His love isn't conditional upon your good actions or holiness. Shift your position to, "God has already provided everything, and if I don't feel His love, it's not that God doesn't love; it's that I don't realize what I have". Begin to change your outcome. Knowing that you have something takes away the struggle. A shift takes place from a legalistic mentality of trying to earn things from God to a child-like faith. It disconnects doubt. How could you ever doubt that you'd get something that you already have?

Philemon 1:6 explains the key connection between the spiritual and material. Paul was praying, "That the communication of thy faith may become effectual"—that means that your faith would begin to work—"by the acknowledging of every good thing which is in you in Christ Jesus". Every good thing is in you in Christ! You've already got it! And Jesus said He would never leave you nor forsake you (Hebrews 13:5). So, instead of praying, "Lord, just be with me this week, if it be Your will..." or "Oh God, where are You? I don't feel Your love God," pray, "Thank You, Father, that You will never leave me, that You're always here. Thank You for Your goodness." Start acknowledging the good things that the Word says are in you, and then your faith begins to be effective. Start seeing these things as apparent in your life. Praising and thanking God is so much easier than begging and pleading with Him.

God has already done His part. When Jesus died on the cross, He said, "It is finished" (John 19:30). And the Scripture reveals in Ephesians 1:20 that He is now seated at the Father's right hand. It is finished!

God already forgave you. He healed you. He commanded His blessing upon you and your finances. He gave you love, joy, and peace. You don't need God to respond to you; you need to learn to respond to God! It's easier to defend something you already have than to get something you don't have.

We need to begin to believe things have happened that we can't see, taste, hear, smell, or feel. We can believe that there are television, radio, and WiFi signals in the atmosphere, even though we can't see them. We know that all we have to do is take a television set, turn it on, and tune it in, and we'll see that those signals were there the whole time. But we need to begin to apply this to spiritual things. We can't limit this concept to our physical realm. This is how you start cooperating with God.

You don't need to try to get God to move in your life. You must instead move into agreement *with* Him and receive what He has provided.

We really cannot fully comprehend the amazing things God has stored up for us; They're already ours. Our challenge to you is not to leave your blessings stored up. Be bold and believe that you're greatly favored, believe that you are well able, believe that you can become all God's created you to be.

We see in 2 Corinthians 1:20 what God says about His promises, "For all the promises of God in Him are Yes, and in Him Amen" (NKJV). God says, "Yes, you're blessed, healthy, strong. Yes, you will accomplish your dreams." But notice they are YES and AMEN. If you want it to become a reality, you've got to add Amen. Amen means, "Be it unto me. God, I agree; Let it happen." It has got to become personal, to take root in your spirit. It's one thing to know that God has blessed; It's another to say, "I am blessed". It's one thing to know that God made you, but it affects you differently when you say, "I am a masterpiece. I am one-of-a-kind. I am fearfully and wonderfully made". God says yes; Make sure you add your Amen to it.

Abraham did this in the Bible. He learned to get in agreement with God. It might have taken about twenty years, but the promise came to pass. I wonder how many blessings have been stored up for us that we missed out on? How many dreams have our name on them, but because we get discouraged that it's taking so long, we settle where we are. We don't see them come to reality.

Go get what already belongs to you. Go get the healing, go get the dreams, go get the victory, all that have your name on them. When you rise up with boldness and say, "God, I know You love me, I know You are good to me. God, I want to thank You for bringing my dreams to pass. Thank You that I'll live healthy and whole, that You're bringing the right people across my path. Lord, thank you for giving me the desires of my heart," you put yourself in alignment with God's promises.

God never created you to reach a certain level and then get stuck; He created you to excel, take new ground for the kingdom, set a new standard for your family. Take the limits off of Him. Get rid of little dreams, little goals, little plans; God wants to show you the greatness of His power. He's not limited by your circumstances, education, background, or talent; We limit God with our thinking. If we think, "I've gone as far as I can, nothing good is in my future. I don't deserve it. I've made too many mistakes," that belief will keep us from the fullness of our destiny. You have to enlarge your vision; make room for God to do something new. He's about to rain down favor, rain down promotion; You're going to see an abundance of His goodness. He's going to take you where you've never been. He's going to show you what you've never seen.

God has big plans for each of us. Ephesians 3:20 declares, "Now to Him who is able to do exceedingly abundantly above all that we ask or think" (NKJV). We often fall into the trap of feeling insignificant in God's design for the world. "God's got bigger things to deal with than me, my challenges, my dreams, or my goals," is commonly heard in our circles. But when we stop listening to the lie and realize, we, creation, are God's biggest deal, the apple of His eye, and His most prized possession, we find our value tucked into His comforting words.

God created you in His own image. He didn't breathe life into the water, the sky, or the trees; He breathed His life into you. He planted His DNA on the inside of you. So you weren't created to be average, or mediocre; You are royalty. God destined you long ago to leave your mark on this generation. Blessings rest on the shelf with your name on them. They already belong to you. God is waiting for you to claim what is rightfully yours. Would you stir up your faith to receive it? Start believing bigger. Start expecting God's goodness, start declaring God's favor. It might not have happened in the past, but this is a new day. It can happen in the future. When you believe, new doors open, promotion comes, the right people show up. When you believe, negative situations begin to turn around. When you believe, all things are possible.

If I have a $100 bill in my hand, that bill does not benefit me in and of itself. In other words, I can't wear the bill; I can't eat the bill; I can't drive the bill. It's simply a piece of paper that's worth hardly anything. But if I take that $100 bill to the store, I can exchange it for groceries or gasoline for my car. Currency is legal tender; That piece of paper can be exchanged for goods and services.

The Bible describes a "legal tender" of sorts, but one used in Heaven. "Now faith is the substance of things hoped for, the evidence of things not seen" (Hebrews 11:1 NKJV). Faith is the currency of Heaven. In the unseen spiritual realm, the substance (currency) needed for exchange is faith.

Abraham wasn't necessarily righteous by our standards. His story is marked with shortcomings and mistakes. Abraham had a baby out of wedlock and lied about his wife, among other things. He didn't live a perfect life, but we see this principle at work: Abraham believed. He had faith. "And he believed the Lord, and he counted it to him as righteousness" (Genesis 15:6 ESV). It is as if God said, "All right, Abraham, you've got the faith, let's make an exchange; I'll give you My righteousness." Faith is what you need to exchange for God's goodness, for His blessing, and for His favor. That's why the scripture says in Hebrews 11:6, "And without faith it is impossible to please God" (NIV). Our lack of faith limits our living in God's provision.

"Yet the Lord longs to be gracious to you..." (Isaiah 30:18 NIV). God wants to bring your dreams to pass, but Isaiah went on to say, "Blessed (happy, fortunate, to be envied) are all those who [earnestly] wait for Him, who expect and look and long for Him [for His victory, His favor, His love, His peace, His joy, and His matchless, unbroken companionship]!" (Isaiah 30:18 AMP). As your faith increases, you have more currency to exchange.

Blessings are activated when we start believing correctly. When you go to God believing big, believing for your dreams, believing that the problem will turn around, knowing that He's all-powerful, that's not just being positive. An exchange is taking place. You're trading your faith, the currency of Heaven; Faith allows God to do amazing things. God says, in effect, "I work by faith; that's the substance I need for the exchange." So we begin to speak the language of faith, "God I've got this big dream, it looks impossible to me, but God, I know with You all things are possible. I know You make a way where I don't see a way. I know You open doors that no man can shut. I know You're supplying my needs according to your riches, not mine. I know you have blessings stored up for me, and all those who love the Lord." And God effectually responds.

Instead of complaining, one of the best things you can do is remind God what He said in His Word. What would happen if we'd all go to God with the currency of Heaven: faith, boldness, confidence, and expectancy? That's what gets God's attention, our knowing that He loves us and He wants to be good to us. That's what releases all that God has for us. Let's stir up our faith. Remember, you're not going to be blessed; you've already been blessed. You're not going to have a crown of favor, you already have a crown a favor; Make sure you put it on each day. God says yes, now add your Amen to it. You're going to see God's goodness in a new way through new opportunities and unfathomable blessings. You're going to step into the fullness of your destiny.

Ponder This:

Examine the types of prayers that you have prayed. What position have they been uttered from?

____

____

____

Practical Practice:

How can you begin to use the currency of Heaven in your life? Start recording how you see a difference in the outcome in your life.

____

____

____

Pray:

God, we thank you that with You all things are possible. We know You can make a way where we don't see a way. We know you have blessings stored up for us. Help us to walk in your ways and see your goodness. Amen.

CHAPTER 9

Guard to Grow

"Carefully guard your thoughts because they are the source of true life." Proverbs 4:23 CEV

A woman in France suffers from heart palpitations, headaches and even seizure-like symptoms. She searched for the cause and was written off as overly dramatic because no physical trace for her symptoms could be found. After much misery, she found the source of her ailments. She was allergic to Wi-Fi signals. Now, it's not polite to laugh. Electromagnetic radiation sensitivity does exist. She happens to have a more severe case than sensitivity, however. She was "attacked" by these unseen waves, and it became debilitating. Enough so, that the French government granted her disability, and she lives remotely without these outside forces. Interesting, isn't it, how the invisible can wield great power? A violent battle is raging around us twenty-four hours per day, as well.

In 1965, Donald Barnhouse wrote a book about it called *The Invisible War*. In the book, he describes a vicious battle for the mind. The battle is severe. It is insistent. And it is unfair, because the enemy of our soul never plays fair. The reason why it is so intense is that your greatest strength is your mind.

Demolishing Strongholds

A simple but often overlooked principle the enemy knows (and uses) is that whatever gets your mind gets you. So one of the most important things we need to learn is how to safeguard, strengthen, and renew our minds, because the fight begins in the mind.

Second Corinthians 10:3-5 (NLT) tells us that "We are human, but we don't wage war as humans do. We use God's mighty weapons, not worldly weapons, to knock down the strongholds of human reasoning and to destroy false arguments. We destroy every proud obstacle that keeps people from knowing God. We capture their rebellious thoughts and teach them to obey Christ". In other words, we don't fight with physical armor, politics, money, or in human ways. Rather we destroy arguments and every lofty opinion and take every thought captive to obey Christ.

The apostle Paul said here that our job in this battle is to "destroy strongholds". Paul was talking about pretentions, influences set up against the knowledge of God. This is a mental battle. A mental block. And he says, "Destroy these strongholds". A stronghold can be a worldview, such as materialism, secularism, relativism, hedonism, or atheism. All of the different -isms are mental strongholds that people set up against the knowledge of God. A stronghold can also be a personal attitude. Anxiety can be a stronghold. Seeking the approval of other people can be a stronghold. Anything that you make an idol in your life can be a stronghold—fear, guilt, resentment, worry, or insecurity. All of these feelings can be strongholds in your mind. The Bible says that we are to tear them down.

Taking Every Thought Captive

Look at the very last phrase in the passage: "take every thought captive to obey Christ". The Greek word *aichmaløtizø* in this scripture means "to control, to conquer, to bring into submission". We conquer. We make thoughts submit. Every thought must be obedient to Christ. Make it obedient. *Hupakøe* means "to bring into submission, to bring under control". Every thought must be brought under the obedience of Christ.

But how do you practically bring your thoughts to the obedience of Christ? Ever notice that your mind doesn't always mind? It is often disobedient. It is often unruly. Minds want to go in different directions from truth. When I want to think a certain way, my mind wants to go another way. When I need to contemplate, it wants to wander. When I need to pray, my thoughts often want to float away.

Paul said, "I do not do the good I want, but the evil I do not want is what I keep on doing. . . . Wretched man that I am!" (Romans 7:19, 24). Even the Apostle Paul wrestled with battling his will.

Four Beliefs for Winning the Battle for Your Mind

The Bible presents many principles for winning the battle of your greatest asset, your mind. Let's uncover four principles for living like Christ, being effective for Him, and claiming your rightful blessings as a believer.

1) Do Not Believe Everything You Think

We logically feel that if we think something, it must be true because it comes from within us. But just because you think something does not make it true. So many different suggestions can come into the mind. The world puts ideas in our minds that are false, and we are barraged with false notions all the time. And, of course, Satan makes recommendations as well. But the real problem lies with the fact that the mind, under the control of sin is: confused (Deuteronomy 28:20), evil and restless (Ecclesiastes 2:21-23), deluded (Isaiah 32:4), and anxious (Job 17:3-4). The Bible talks about a corrupt mind (2 Timothy 3:8), a depraved mind (1 Timothy 6:5), a blinded mind (2 Corinthians 4:4), a troubled mind (2 Kings 6:11), and a sinful mind (Romans 8:7), to name a few. The mind is a key area of focus throughout scripture, and when we learn to align our thoughts with God's purposes, His best for us begins to unfold in our lives.

Our Broken Minds

Our minds are broken by sin, which means we cannot trust even what we think ourselves. Jeremiah 17:9 says, "The heart is deceitful above all things, and desperately wicked; who can know it?" (NKJV). We have an amazing ability to lie to ourselves.

That's why you need to question your own thoughts. Just because you get a thought doesn't mean it's right. Sin begins with a lie. The Bible says Satan is "the father of lies" (John 8:44). And if he can get you to believe a lie, he can get you to sin. Anytime you sin, you are thinking that you know better than God. God said one thing, but we wonder if there is a better way? And so you have to question what you think. First John 1:8 tells us, "If we say we have no sin, we deceive ourselves, and the truth is not in us" (KJV). We deceive ourselves.

2) Shield Your Mind from Trash

The second thing to learn in this battle for the mind is to shield your mind from trash. The old cliché from the computer's early days—GIGO, garbage in/garbage out—is still true today. If you put bad files into a computer, you will get corrupt results. If you put mental garbage into your mind, you will get junk out in your life. "A wise person is hungry for knowledge, while the fool feeds on trash" (Proverbs 15:14 NLT). What a great verse to remember and use often in our lives.

I took a nutrition course in college and remember the professor telling us there were basically three kinds of food in the way of nourishment for our bodies. Brain food that helps your brain operate proficiently, junk food that is empty calories, not beneficial or nutritious to the body, and toxic foods, which have negative effects and are a slow poison of sorts for the system.

We can apply this principle to our spiritual nourishment as well—what we see, what we hear, and what we allow into our minds. Some sustenance is soul food. It will make you wiser, more godly, and more emotionally mature. Then there is junk food. You can fill your mind with so much that is just padding. It is neither bad nor good, as 1 Corinthians 6:12 says, permissible but not beneficial. In other words, some things aren't necessarily wrong, they just aren't necessary. Then there are toxic thoughts, negative thoughts that poison our spirits. The Bible tells us to fill our minds with the right things. If you want to be healthy and blessed in your Christian life, fill your mind with the right things.

Faithful and Fruitful

For those who believe God hasn't called them to be successful, but rather only to be faithful; that's not fully true. God expects not only faithfulness but also fruitfulness. Trace it through Scriptures. John 15:16 tells us, "I chose you . . . that you should go and bear fruit". Faithfulness is only half the equation. God anticipates fruitfulness as well.

Psalm 101:3 instructs us to, "... not set before my eyes anything that is worthless". As unimaginable as it would be for us to invite a couple to commit an act of adultery in our living room, we do that every time we watch a TV program that has adultery in it. You would never invite someone to murder another in your presence, but murderous scenes are so commonplace in our entertainment, some of us are offended if that kind of drama isn't in our programming. Sometimes we are tricked into thinking that we can allow anything into our minds without any negative effects. Don't be fooled, we get out what we put in.

Ways to Guard Our Minds

Philippians 4:6-8 gives some great tools to help us guard our minds. "Do not be anxious about anything, but in everything by prayer and supplication with thanksgiving let your requests be made known to God. And the peace of God, which surpasses all understanding, will guard your hearts and your minds in Christ Jesus. Finally, brothers, whatever is true, whatever is honorable, whatever is just, whatever is pure, whatever is lovely, whatever is commendable, if there is any excellence, if there is anything worthy of praise, think about these things."

We see two weapons to pack in our arsenal here: conversational, continual prayer and concentrated, intentional focus. The first tool to guard your heart and mind is "in everything" to pray. Then Paul says to think about "whatever is true, whatever is honorable, whatever is just, whatever is pure, whatever is lovely, whatever is commendable, if there is any excellence, if there is anything worthy of praise". Notice that he says to pray about everything. If we were to pray as much as worry, wouldn't we have a lot less reason to worry? Consider every worry an opportunity to pray. Prayer then becomes less of a pious duty and more a heartfelt interaction.

How do you know when you have the peace that "surpasses all understanding"? When you give up trying to comprehend fully why God does what He does and simply release in trust to Him. This peace "will guard your hearts and your minds".

Intentional prayer takes purpose, in that we have been taught to pray a "certain" way, but God's design was far more relational. Talk to God at all times, in doing so you are in effect praying about everything. Keep a running dialog with your caring Creator.

Second, Paul said that we should fix our thoughts. "Think about these things." How do you do that? By determined focusing. This is one of the keys to overpowering temptation: Don't merely repel it; replace it. Whatever you merely resist persists. When someone says, "I don't want to think about this," what are they actually doing? They are thinking about it! And whatever you focus on grows. The book of James tells us that "Sin when it is fully grown brings forth death" (James 1:15). So don't merely resist it; replace it. Change the channel. Refocus. Think on the things he instructs us in Philippians as suitable replacements.

3) Never Stop Learning

The third thing to learn in this battle for the mind is to never stop learning. Become a lifetime learner. Love wisdom. Love knowledge. Learn to love the act of learning. The word disciple means "learner". You cannot be a disciple of Christ without being a student. Jesus said, "Come to me, all who labor and are heavy laden, and I will give you rest. Take my yoke upon you, and learn from me" (Matthew 11:28-19). Jesus wants us to learn from Him.

Many people act as though their learning ended at their last graduation. They have never studied anything else. They have never taken another class since leaving school. However, to be a disciple means to be a learner. All leaders must first be disciples. So leaders must first be learners. The moment you stop learning, you stop growing because stagnation leads to futility.

You can learn from anybody if you simply discover how to draw out his or her knowledge. And how do you do it? You draw knowledge from others by asking questions. The Bible says, "Counsel in the heart of man is like deep water; but a man of understanding will draw it out" (Proverbs 20:5 KJV). Each of us knows something that others don't, and others know things of which we are ignorant. You can glean knowledge from anybody if you just know the right questions. That's why the Bible says, "Iron sharpens iron" (Proverbs 27:17).

Humility is Needed

Humility is the fundamental component to learning. Why does God resist the proud and give grace to the humble (1Peter 5:5)? Simply because the humble are teachable. I would rather admit that I don't know it all than pretend I know it all and not learn. You can learn from anybody. The real question is are you humble enough to receive from others?

We can learn from those older or younger than ourselves. We can learn from our critics and our mentors. Proverbs 18:15 says, "The mind of a person who has understanding acquires knowledge. The ears of wise people seek knowledge"(GW). We need to be eager to learn and willing to listen.

Proverbs 10:14 says, "Wise men store up knowledge" (NIV). In Scripture, we are instructed not to store up earthly things. However, knowledge is one thing we are supposed to store up. Don't store up material possessions where moth and rust decay, but store up knowledge because knowledge is far more important than treasure.

No Failure

What would you attempt for God if you knew you couldn't fail? "And in the last days it shall be, God declares, that I will pour out my Spirit on all flesh, and your sons and your daughters shall prophesy, and your young men shall see visions, and your old men shall dream dreams" (Acts 2:17 ESV). What's your dream for your next ten years? Have you written that dream down? Thoughts become clear when they go through the lips and the fingertips. If you haven't written it down, you haven't really thought about it. Writing makes a dream more precise. What is your dream for your family? What is your personal dream? How are you going to be different ten years from now? What we need today are people who imagine great possibilities.

We can only do the impossible if we perceive the invisible. God cannot fulfill your dream if you don't have one. God cannot bless your vision if you don't have

His vision for your life. God cannot help you reach a goal if you don't have purpose.

A goal is a statement of faith, of sorts. "Without faith it is impossible to please God" (Hebrews 11:6), and "whatever does not proceed from faith is sin" (Romans 14:23). The Bible says that "according to your faith be it done to you" (Matthew 9:29). So when we set goals, we are effectually saying, *God, I believe you want me to accomplish this with your help by this time*. Dream great dreams for God, and teach others to dream great dreams for God.

It's not enough just not to believe everything we think. It's not enough just to guard our minds from garbage. It's not enough to keep on learning and developing character. We must also let God develop our imaginations and plant seeds of great dreams into our hearts. Because we must outthink and out-dream and outsmart the world for the glory of God—not for our private good but for the glory of God and the good of others.

Paul said in Ephesians 3:20, "Now to him who is able to do far more abundantly than all that we ask or think"—more than we can imagine. More than we can dream. Infinitely beyond our highest prayers, aspirations, thoughts, or hopes.

THINK!

Remember this acrostic to quickly remember how to claim all that is yours as a Christian: THINK. Five things to remember in our own lives and to teach others. Five things to guard and grow and bless and be blessed.

T - *Test every thought.* "Search me, O God, and know my heart! Try me and know my thoughts! And see if there be any grievous way in me, and lead me in the way everlasting!" (Psalm 139:23-24). Ask God to test and search your thoughts. Don't believe everything you think. Test every thought.

H - *Helmet your head.* Put on the helmet of salvation. You can't ride a motorcycle without wearing a helmet. Why? Because if you hurt your head, you are in deep trouble. And the Bible says, "Take the helmet of salvation" (Ephesians 6:17). Until we have salvation, we don't have any protection against the fiery darts that the Devil releases on our minds. Repentance means changing your mind—not just changing what you do. It's a heart and mind change. Repentance is changing the way you think, a mental shift. Put on the helmet of salvation.

I - *Imagine great thoughts*. Everything is possible to him who believes (Mark 9:23). Think about all of God's great promises. What an amazing blank check we have in Christ. Imagine great thoughts. Use these great thoughts to replace negative thoughts.

N - *Nourish a godly mind*. Make sure that you are growing and developing. Psalm 119:15 says, "I will meditate on your precepts and fix my eyes on your ways." Meditate and fix your eyes on God's ways. Study and reflect.

K - *Keep learning*. The Bible says, "Practice these things, immerse yourself in them, so that all may see your progress" (1 Timothy 4:15). Do others see progress in your life? Are your words and conversations more powerful, deeper, stronger, more practical, more life-touching since you began to implement these principles?

The Christian life is not just knowing; It's being and doing, being blessed and being a blessing.

Ponder This:

What are some ways you can intentionally grow in knowledge? How can you implement some of these into your life?

____

____

____

Practical Practice:

We need to become great, godly dreamers. Proverbs 29:18 is about vision for our lives. The word "vision" relates to dreaming. And when this God-directed dreaming is missing, the people "cast off restraint"—literally, they get "out of control". When we do not have an overarching vision for our lives, our lives are out of control. What dream has God placed in you?

____

____

____

Pray:

Heavenly Father, thank you that your vision and dreams for us are far greater than we can imagine. May we be transformed by the renewing of our minds so that we may know your will—which is good and pleasing and perfect. In Jesus's name we pray. Amen.

CONCLUSION

The Weight on the Wicker Chair

Walking into this fancy tea room was not what I was accustomed to. I have never been the frou-frou type. Although I appreciate and enjoy fine china and beautiful décor, I am much more low maintenance. But a dear friend wanted to do something special for me and treating me to her favorite place was the perfect way to connect and celebrate our birthdays. I had been carrying around some extra baby weight on an already heavy frame and remember having to navigate the tight spaces to get to our table with a prayer muttered under my breath that my girth wouldn't break anything. This place was packed! I could only imagine how much these delicate surroundings cost, and I did not want to draw attention to what I felt certain everyone else saw as the sore thumb sticking out, or the elephant in the room. I was the heaviest I had ever been and every waking moment my thoughts revolved around that fact. If only I could lose this weight. If only. I could finally stop the judgmental glances, whispered comments and stares of disgust. Then I would finally measure up.

We were led to a lovely table covered in white lace and table dressings I had never been introduced to before. And we sat down. The chairs were wicker, and I heard an ominous creek as soon as the burden of my body settled into the chair's embrace. I ignored it foolishly, optimistically thinking it was nothing, and looked at the menu of delicacies, calculating calories and taste in a flash. My thoughts were interrupted by a louder crack followed by a crash, and before I could do anything I was on the floor—skirt raised, awkwardly positioned, and hurt. Physically and emotionally anguished. A kind gesture had quickly turned into a horrible nightmare. I was humiliated. I didn't eat that day, despite my friend's fight with the manager about how flimsy the chairs were and the onslaught of attention it brought. I was mortified. I quickly covered my feelings with laughter to conceal the volcano of emotion that was about to erupt and made fun of myself and the situation. But I silently prayed to change. Mine was a desperate prayer.

And change I did. One hundred pounds, lost. Tenaciously over a year, I worked hard for that loss, but I remained empty inside. A deeper longing that could not be filled with earthly gains (or losses)—nagged at me like hunger pangs.

Pursuing our own will and things we perceive to fill us will always leave us pining. The list of things we reason will fix us goes well beyond weight loss, relationships and blessings. I'm sure you could add to this list. Life is not neat and tidy. There are letdowns and hurts enough to harden the softest hearts. These things are just part of life. But Jesus doesn't refuse to reach out to us in the middle of hurts and heartbreaks, mess-ups, and broken wicker chairs. Our Lord's holiness has never been hesitant to step into the haze of humanity. He is the great answer to our *every* desire. And He will not let our need for divine profound love, meant to be fulfilled by Him alone, cheaply be met by inadequate means.

Second Peter 2:19 (NLT) states, "For you are a slave to whatever controls you". It all comes back to what we worship. God is not going to take second place in our lives. In order to live a life filled with His goodness, we must seek Him first. We must make Him

Lord over every area of our lives.

He might very well give us good gifts. He might entrust with us relationships and success and blessings of all kinds. After all, He loves to give good gifts to those He loves. But He will not honor the chase of pursuing our own wills. If we think lesser things can truly satisfy, we will forever chase the wind. It is an exhausting search. We will forever be in hot pursuit of becoming someone we believe we need to be. One day I will become someone's spouse, one day I will become someone significant. One day I will live there, or drive that, or be able to buy things without looking at the price tags. One day I will lose this weight. One day I will hit this standard of success or skill or status. We dream it with such confidence and then pursue everything and everyone that can help us reach our worldly goals. In the process, we run farther and farther away from the only giver of good gifts, the one who wants to live a love story with us. Not like the magic genie we run to for the occasional dose of divine help, but the one who stills us, fills our emptiness and wipes away our tired striving and whispers, "It's not about you becoming anything. Your soul was made simply to be with Me. And the more you are with Me, the more you will stop fearing what the world might take from you. With Me you are free to be you. The *real* you. The you whose core is in alignment with my truth. The you who doesn't fear imperfections or rejections, because grace has covered those in the loveliest of ways." With Jesus we are forever safe, complete, and completely loved. Blessed.

Bonus
SECTION

100 Blessings for the Believer from the Bible

"God be gracious to us and bless us" (Psalm 67:1a). Do you pray that often for yourself, your marriage, your children, and for the church? We all desperately need God's grace and His blessing. God's grace is one of the most basic concepts to grasp if you want to experience His blessing, and yet it is not easy to grasp in practice because grace runs contrary to our sense of fairness and justice. All aspects of life program us to work hard to earn what we get. But God's grace humbles our pride, saying, "You deserve My judgment, but I'm going to give you My favor."

Grace means we get blessings that we do not deserve. We can't earn grace or it becomes a wage, not grace (Romans 4:4-5). We deserve God's judgment for our sins, but He gives us a free pardon and eternal life through Jesus Christ, who paid our debt. The Christian life from beginning to end depends on God's grace. We received Christ because of God's grace; we walk in God's grace (Colossians 2:6). We enjoy all of God's blessings because of His grace that He ordained for us in Christ (Ephesians 1:3-6).

By God's blessing, I'm referring to His favor, goodness, joy, or well-being bestowed on us.

God's blessings encompass the total well-being that comes from being the object of His favor. Blessings may be material, such as good health and adequate financial provisions. They include harmonious relationships in our families and peace with others. But the greatest blessings are spiritual, because blessings are eternal. In that sense, Paul said in Ephesians 1:3, "Blessed be the God and Father of our Lord Jesus Christ, who has blessed us with every spiritual blessing in the heavenly places in Christ." If we have eternal spiritual blessings, then we are blessed even if we suffer. As 1 Peter 4:14 says, "If you are reviled for the name of Christ, you are blessed, because the Spirit of glory and of God rests on you."

Here are some of our favorite promises and blessings for you to begin to affirm in your life.

1) God blesses us so we can be a blessing to others! *"I will cause my people and their homes around my holy hill to BE a blessing. And I will send showers, showers of blessings, which will come just when they are needed."* (Ezekiel 34:26 NLT)
2) We are blessed in EVERY way! *"You will be blessed in every way, and you will be able to keep on being generous. Then many people will thank God when we deliver your gift."* (2 Corinthians 9:11 CEV)
3) The blessing of being adopted by God. *"To redeem them that were under the law, that we might receive the adoption of sons."* (Galatians 4:5 KJV)
4) The blessing of an inheritance. *"In whom also we have obtained an inheritance, being predestinated according to the purpose of him who worketh all things after the counsel of his own will."* (Ephesians 1:11 KJV)
5) It's never too late to start living a God-blessed life! *"So the LORD blessed Job in the second half of his life even more than in the beginning."* (Job 42:12 NLT)

6) Blessed to access God's grace. *"For by grace are ye saved through faith; and that not of yourselves: it is the gift of God: For through him we both have access by one Spirit unto the Father."* (Ephesians 2:8, 18 KJV)

7) The blessing that comes from daily meeting with God. *"Blessed is the one who listens to me, watching daily at my gates, waiting beside my doors."* (Proverbs 8:34 ESV)

8) We become a child of God. *"But as many as received him, to them gave he power to become the sons of God, even to them that believe on his name."* (John 1:12 KJV)

9) The blessing of being reconciled to God. *"For if, when we were enemies, we were reconciled to God by the death of his Son, much more, being reconciled, we shall be saved by his life."* (Romans 5:10 KJV)

10) The blessing of having peace with God. *"Peace I leave with you, my peace I give unto you: not as the world giveth, give I unto you. Let not your heart be troubled, neither let it be afraid."* (John 14:27 KJV)

11) The blessing for those who obey God's instruction. *"Whoever gives heed to instruction prospers, and blessed is he who trusts in the Lord."* (Proverbs 16:20 NIV)

12) The blessing that comes from tithing. *"Bring the whole tithe into the storehouse, that there may be food in my house. Test me in this," says the Lord Almighty, "and see if I will not throw open the floodgates of heaven and pour out so much blessing that you will not have room enough to store it."* (Malachi 3:10 NIV)

13) The blessing of attributed righteousness. *"Even as David also describeth the blessedness of the man, unto whom God imputeth righteousness without works."* (Romans 4:6 KJV)

14) We have been delivered from the power of darkness. *"Giving thanks unto the Father, which hath made us meet to be partakers of the inheritance of the saints in light: Who hath delivered us from the power of darkness, and hath translated us into the kingdom of his dear Son."* (Colossians 1:12-13 KJV)

15) God promises to bless our life if we share the Good News. *"I pray you will be active in sharing your faith, so that you will fully understand every blessing we have in Christ."* (Philemon 1:6 NIV)

16) The blessing of having all our needs supplied by God's riches in glory. *"But my God shall supply all your need according to his riches in glory by Christ Jesus."* (Philippians 4:19 KJV)

17) Blessing for the generous. *"For those who are always generous and lend freely, their children will be blessed."* (Psalm 37:26 NIV)

18) The blessing of being in the Lamb's book of life. *"And there shall in no wise enter into it any thing that defileth, neither whatsoever worketh abomination, or maketh a lie: but they which are written in the Lamb's book of life."* (Revelation 21:27 KJV)

19) The blessing of the anointing. *"But the anointing which ye have received of him abideth in you, and ye need not that any man teach you: but as the same anointing teacheth you of all things, and is truth, and is no lie, and*

even as it hath taught you, ye shall abide in him." (1 John 2:27 KJV)

20) The blessing of being forever forgiven. *"Then he adds: 'Their sins and lawless acts I will remember no more.'"* (Hebrews 10:17 NIV)

21) The blessing granted if we assist the poor and the helpless. *"Blessed is he that considereth the poor: the LORD will deliver him in time of trouble. The LORD will preserve him, and keep him alive; and he shall be blessed upon the earth: and thou wilt not deliver him unto the will of his enemies."* (Psalm 41:1-2 KJV)

22) The blessing of inner strength to accomplish necessary things. *"I can do all things through Christ which strengtheneth me."* (Philippians 4:13 KJV)

23) The blessing for spreading the gospel. *"The one who plants and the one who waters have one purpose, and they will each be rewarded according to their own labor."* (1 Corinthians 3:8 NIV)

24) The blessing of not having a spirit of fear. *"For God hath not given us the spirit of fear;*

but of power, and of love, and of a sound mind." (2 Timothy 1:7 KJV)

25) Blessed by being a priest in His kingdom. *"And hath made us kings and priests unto God and his Father; to him be glory and dominion for ever and ever. Amen."*
(Revelation 1:6 KJV)

26) The blessing of being sealed by the Holy Spirit unto the day of redemption. *"And grieve not the Holy Spirit of God, whereby ye are sealed unto the day of redemption."*
(Ephesians 4:30 KJV)

27) God promises to bless our lives if we study and act upon His Word. *"Blessed is the man... whose delight is in the law of the Lord, and on his word he meditates day and night. He is like a tree planted by streams of water, which yields its fruit in season and whose leaf does not wither. Whatever he does prospers."*
(Psalm 1:1-3 NIV)

28) The blessing of being complete in Christ. *"And ye are complete in him, which is the head of all principality and power."*
(Colossians 2:10 KJV)

29) The blessing on our food and health when we worship. *"Worship the Lord your God and his blessing will be on your food and water. I will take away sickness from among you."* (Exodus 23:25 NIV)

30) The blessing of being heirs of God, joint heirs with Jesus. *"And if children, then heirs; heirs of God, and joint-heirs with Christ; if so be that we suffer with him, that we may be also glorified together."* (Romans 8:17 KJV)

31) The blessing of heavenly citizenship. *"And the Lord shall deliver me from every evil work, and will preserve me unto his heavenly kingdom: to whom be glory for ever and ever. Amen."* (2 Timothy 4:18 KJV)

32) The blessing of becoming a friend of God. *"Henceforth I call you not servants; for the servant knoweth not what his lord doeth: but I have called you friends; for all things that I have heard of my Father I have made known unto you."* (John 15:15 KJV)

33) The blessing from hearing and practicing the Word. *"Even more blessed are all who hear the*

word of God and put it into practice." (Luke 11:28 NLT)

34) The blessing from sharing. "*A generous man will himself be blessed, for he shares his food with the poor.*" (Proverbs 22:9 NIV)

35) The blessing of sanctification. "*And such were some of you: but ye are washed, but ye are sanctified, but ye are justified in the name of the Lord Jesus, and by the Spirit of our God.*" (1 Corinthians 6:11 KJV)

36) The blessing of being joined unto the Lord. "*But he that is joined unto the Lord is one spirit.*" (1 Corinthians 6:17 KJV)

37) Blessed by having our names written in Heaven. "*Notwithstanding in this rejoice not, that the spirits are subject unto you; but rather rejoice, because your names are written in heaven.*" (Luke 10:20 KJV)

38) The blessing bestowed on our children. You can create a legacy. "*After Abraham's death, God poured out rich blessings on Isaac.*" (Genesis 25:11 NLT)

39) The blessing of becoming a new creature. "*Therefore if any man be in Christ, he is a new*

creature: old things are passed away; behold, all things are become new." (2 Corinthians 5:17 KJV)

40) The blessing of having an advocate in Christ. *"My little children, these things write I unto you, that ye sin not. And if any man sin, we have an advocate with the Father, Jesus Christ the righteous."* (1 John 2:1 KJV)

41) The blessing of being a worker with God. "*We then, as workers together with him, beseech you also that ye receive not the grace of God in vain."* (2 Corinthians 6:1 KJV)

42) The blessing of being accepted in the Beloved. *"To the praise of the glory of his grace, wherein he hath made us accepted in the beloved."* (Ephesians 1:6 KJV)

43) The blessing if we participate in fellowship with other believers. *"I'm eager to encourage you in your faith, but I also want to be encouraged by yours. In this way, each of us will be a blessing to the other."* (Romans 1:12 NLT)

44) The blessing of life eternal. *"And I give unto them eternal life; and they shall never perish,*

neither shall any man pluck them out of my hand." (John 10:28 KJV)

45) The blessing of becoming a humble servant of God. "*But now being made free from sin, and become servants to God, ye have your fruit unto holiness, and the end everlasting life.*" (Romans 6:22 KJV)

46) We are given a blessed hope of Christ's return. "*Looking for that blessed hope, and the glorious appearing of the great God and our Saviour Jesus Christ.*" (Titus 2:13 KJV)

47) The blessing of having the Holy Spirit abide in us. "*But ye are not in the flesh, but in the Spirit, if so be that the Spirit of God dwell in you. Now if any man have not the Spirit of Christ, he is none of his.*" (Romans 8:9 KJV)

48) The blessing of obeying God. "*Happy are those who respect the Lord and obey him. You will enjoy what you work for, and you will be blessed with good things.*"
(Psalm 128:1-2 NCV)

49) The blessing of our Heavenly mansion. "*In my Father's house are many mansions: if it were*

not so, I would have told you. I go to prepare a place for you." (John 14:2 KJV)

50) The blessing of spiritual birth. We are born again with a spiritual re-birth. *"Jesus answered and said unto him, Verily, verily, I say unto thee, Except a man be born again, he cannot see the kingdom of God. Nicodemus saith unto him, How can a man be born when he is old? Can he enter the second time into his mother's womb, and be born? Jesus answered, Verily, verily, I say unto thee, Except a man be born of water and of the Spirit, he cannot enter into the kingdom of God. That which is born of the flesh is flesh; and that which is born of the Spirit is spirit."* (John 3:3-6 KJV)

51) The blessing of being able to put on Christ. *"For as many of you as have been baptized into Christ have put on Christ."*
(Galatians 3:27 KJV)

52) The blessing of being anointed by God. *"Now He who establishes us with you in Christ and anointed us is God."*
(2 Corinthians 1:21 NASB)

53) The blessing for those who persevere. *"Blessed is the man who perseveres under trial, because when he has stood the test, he will receive the crown of life that God has promised to those who love him."* (James 1:12 NIV)

54) The blessing on our work. *"Give freely to the poor person, and do not wish that you didn't have to give. The Lord your God will bless your work and everything you touch."* (Deuteronomy 15:10 NCV)

55) The blessing of protection. *"Blessed is he who has regard for the weak; the Lord delivers him in times of trouble. The Lord will protect him and preserve his life; he will bless him in the land and not surrender him to the desire of his foes."* (Psalm 41:1-2 NIV)

56) The promise that God will turn all things to our good. *"And we know that all things work together for good to them that love God, to them who are the called according to his purpose."* (Romans 8:28 KJV)

57) The blessing in wisdom. *"Blessed is the man who finds wisdom and gains understanding."* (Proverbs 3:13 NIV)

58) The promise to complete a good work in us. *"Being confident of this very thing, that he which hath begun a good work in you will perform it until the day of Jesus Christ."* (Philippians 1:6 KJV)

59) The blessing of wealth without added trouble. *"The blessing of the Lord brings wealth, and he adds no trouble to it."* (Proverbs 10:22 NIV)

60) The blessing in the correction. *"Blessed is the man whom God corrects; so do not despise the discipline of the Almighty."* (Job 5:17 NIV)

61) The blessing in waiting on God. *"The Lord longs to be gracious to you; he rises to show you compassion. For the Lord is a God of justice, blessed are all who wait for him!"* (Isaiah 30:18 NIV)

62) The blessing of being justified in God's sight. *"Therefore being justified by faith, we have peace with God through our Lord Jesus Christ."* (Romans 5:1 KJV)

63) The blessing for the faithful. *"A faithful man will be richly blessed, but one eager to get rich will not go unpunished."* (Proverbs 28:20 NIV)

64) The promise to be able to resist temptation. *"There hath no temptation taken you but such as is common to man: but God is faithful, who will not suffer you to be tempted above that ye are able; but will with the temptation also make a way to escape, that ye may be able to bear it."* (1 Corinthians 10:13 KJV)

65) Blessing for those who realize their need for God. *"Blessed are the poor in spirit, for theirs is the kingdom of heaven."* (Matthew 5:3 NIV)

66) The blessing for those who mourn. *"Blessed are those who mourn, for they will be comforted."* (Matthew 5:4 NIV)

67) A blessing for the humble. *"Blessed are the meek, for they will inherit the earth."* (Matthew 5:5 NIV)

68) The blessing for the seekers of righteousness. *"Blessed are those who hunger and thirst for righteousness, for they will be filled."* (Matthew 5:6 NIV)

69) The blessing for those who are merciful. *"Blessed are the merciful, for they will be shown mercy."* (Matthew 5:7 NIV)

70) The blessing for those who keep their hearts pure. *"Blessed are the pure in heart, for they will see God."* (Matthew 5:8 NIV)

71) A blessing for the peacemakers. *"Blessed are the peacemakers, for they will be called sons of God."* (Matthew 5:9 NIV)

72) The blessing for those who are persecuted. *"Blessed are those who are persecuted because of righteousness, for theirs is the kingdom of heaven."* (Matthew 5:10 NIV)

73) A blessing for those who have been insulted because of their faith. *"Blessed are you when people insult you, persecute you and falsely say all kinds of evil against you because of me."* (Matthew 5:11 NIV)

74) The blessing of the mind of Christ. *"For, 'Who can know the LORD's thoughts? Who knows enough to teach him?' But we understand these things, for we have the mind of Christ."* (1 Corinthians 2 :16 NLT)

75) The blessing for those who do not walk in wicked ways. *"Blessed is the man who does not walk in the counsel of the wicked, nor stand in*

the path of sinners, nor sit in the seat of scoffers!" (Psalm 1:1 NASB)

76) The blessing of pleasant years on earth. *"If they listen and obey God, then they will be blessed with prosperity throughout their lives. All their years will be pleasant."* (Job 36:11 NLT)

77) The blessing of being called out of darkness. *"But ye are a chosen generation, a royal priesthood, an holy nation, a peculiar people; that ye should show forth the praises of him who hath called you out of darkness into his marvellous light."* (1 Peter 2:9 KJV)

78) We are blessed with spiritual blessings. *"Blessed be the God and Father of our Lord Jesus Christ, who hath blessed us with all spiritual blessings in heavenly places in Christ."* (Ephesians 1:3 KJV)

79) A blessing for those who suffer. *"Even if you should suffer for what is right, you will be blessed."* (1 Peter 3:14 NIV)

80) A promise of God's presence for the insulted. *"If you are insulted because of the name of Christ, you are blessed, for the Spirit of glory and of God rests on you."* (1 Peter 4:14 NIV)

81) A blessing for those who embrace wisdom. *"Blessed is the man who finds wisdom, the man who gains understanding, for she is more profitable than silver and yields better returns than gold. She is more precious than rubies; nothing you desire can compare with her. Long life is in her right hand; in her left hand are riches and honor. Her ways are pleasant ways, and all her paths are peace. She is a tree of life to those who embrace her; those who lay hold of her will be blessed."* (Proverbs 3:13-18 NIV)

82) A blessing for those who believe without seeing. *"Jesus said, 'Blessed are those who have not seen me and yet have believed.'"* (John 20:29 NIV)

83) A blessed heritage. *"The memory of the righteous will be a blessing."*
(Proverbs 10:7 NIV)

84) A blessing for those who maintain justice. *"Blessed are they who maintain justice, who constantly do what is right."* (Psalm 106:3 NIV)

85) The blessing for the pursuers of love and righteousness. *"He who pursues righteousness*

and love finds life, prosperity and honor.” (Proverbs 21:21 NIV)

86) The blessing of victory over sin. *“For sin shall not have dominion over you: for ye are not under the law, but under grace.”* (Romans 6:14 KJV)

87) The blessing of being Christ’s ambassadors. *“Now then we are ambassadors for Christ, as though God did beseech you by us: we pray you in Christ’s stead, be ye reconciled to God.”* (2 Corinthians 5:20 KJV)

88) A special blessing for those who fear the Lord. *“Blessed is the man who fears the Lord, who finds great delight in his commands. His children will be mighty in the land; the generation of the upright will be blessed. Wealth and riches are in his house, and his righteousness endures forever.”* (Psalm 112:1-3 NIV)

89) Blessings for the upright and big-hearted. *“Good people will be generous to others and will be blessed for all they do.”* (Isaiah 32:8 NLT)

90) Blessed to spread God's name to the ends of the earth. *"God will bless us, and all the ends of the earth will fear Him."* (Psalm 67:7 HCSB)

91) Blessed member of the body of Christ. *"Now ye are the body of Christ, and members in particular."* (1 Corinthians 12:27 KJV)

92) A blessing for those who know and do. *"If you know these things, you are blessed if you do them."* (John 13:17 NASB)

93) A promised faithfulness regardless of our faithlessness. *"If we believe not, yet he abideth faithful: he cannot deny himself."* (2 Timothy 2:13 KJV)

94) The blessing of redemption. *"And they sung a new song, saying, Thou art worthy to take the book, and to open the seals thereof: for thou wast slain, and hast redeemed us to God by thy blood out of every kindred, and tongue, and people, and nation."* (Revelation 5:9 KJV)

95) A blessing for those who are kind to the needy. *"He who despises his neighbor sins, but blessed is he who is kind to the needy."* (Proverbs 14:21 NIV)

96) The blessing of abounding grace. *"And God is able to make all grace abound toward you; that ye, always having all sufficiency in all things, may abound to every good work."* (2 Corinthians 9:8 KJV)

97) The blessing of being God's workmanship. *"For we are his workmanship, created in Christ Jesus unto good works, which God hath before ordained that we should walk in them."* (Ephesians 2:10 KJV)

98) A blessing for those who return to the Almighty. *"If you return to the Almighty, you will be blessed again. So remove evil from your house."* (Job 22:23 NCV)

99) The blessing of the Lord as our helper. *"So that we may boldly say, The Lord is my helper, and I will not fear what man shall do unto me."* (Hebrews 13:6 KJV)

100) An extensive blessing for the obedient. *"Obey the Lord your God so that all these blessings will come and stay with you: You will be blessed in the city and blessed in the country. Your children will be blessed, as well as your crops; your herds will be blessed with calves*

> *and your flocks with lambs. Your basket and your kitchen will be blessed. You will be blessed when you come in and when you go out. The Lord will help you defeat the enemies that come to fight you. They will attack you from one direction, but they will run from you in seven directions. The Lord will bless you with full barns, and he will bless everything you do."* (Deuteronomy 28:2-8 NCV)

His blessings are gracious, in that we can't earn them. He gives His greatest blessing of salvation freely to the undeserving. But if we reject that blessing or respond to His kindness with defiance or disobedience, we can't expect His blessing. He blesses those who obey Him.

The only source we have for knowing about Jesus Christ so that we can believe in Him is the written testimony of the apostles contained in the New Testament. Of course, the entire Old Testament pointed ahead to Christ (Luke 24:27, 44), but those truths can be understood adequately only through the lens of the New

Testament testimony to Christ. The Holy Spirit inspired the biblical writers to record truthfully all that we need to know about Jesus Christ so that we may believe in Him and be saved.

The Word, not our feelings, is the source of truth about Jesus.

This truth is liberating. When you understand that the blessings of God's grace come only through faith in Christ, the knowledge is humbling, but it is liberating as well "For you have been called to live in freedom" (Galations 5:13a NLT).

So how can we receive God's blessings? They are possible only as presented to us by God as a gift and through the person of Jesus Christ.

We were, after all saved, "by grace, through faith" and we must live "by grace, through faith." This is the way to blessing.

When you receive Christ, you are not only redeemed from something, but you are also redeemed for something.

You were forgiven so that you might be filled. The ultimate blessing is God living in you in grace. The promise of the Spirit means that you can practice the presence of Christ, the character of Christ, and develop the fruit of the Spirit if you will.

Is God's blessing, received through faith in Christ, the source of your strength?

We must know that only by Him are blessings possible. Only through the work of the cross and the indwelling of the Holy Spirit can we receive His blessings. Will we be able to recognize the work of God in our lives?

Are you certain of these things in your life? This is an opportunity to be sure. Go before the Lord in prayer and seek to understand the blessings of God.

He has freed us from our sin, He has freed us from the law, and now he asks only that we trust Him and obey. He even provides us the strength to fulfill His requests.

Will you trust God as you pray these blessings in your life? Record your first prayer on the following page.

www.ingramcontent.com/pod-product-compliance
Lightning Source LLC
Chambersburg PA
CBHW072004040426
42447CB00009B/1484

9780998399904